NEW VISTAS

1

STUDENT BOOK

H. DOUGLAS BROWN

ANNE ALBARELLI-SIEGFRIED

FEDERICO SALAS

ALICE SAVAGE • MASOUD SHAFIEI

Internet Activities by
Dave Sperling and Leeann Iracane

Longman

Library of Congress Cataloging–in–Publication Data

Brown, H. Douglas, 1941–
     New vistas, Student book 1 / H. Douglas Brown.
          p.   cm.
     ISBN 0–13–908195–X
     1. English language– – Textbooks for foreign speakers.   I.   Title.
PE1128.B7248   1999
428.2'4--dc21
                                                                98-14842
                                                                CIP

Publisher: *Mary Jane Peluso*
Series Editor: *Stella Reilly*
Development Editor: *Margaret Grant*
Editorial Assistant: *Alison Kinney*
Director of Production
    and Manufacturing: *Aliza Greenblatt*
Production/Design Manager-Multimedia: *Paul Belfanti*
Electronic Production Editor: *Carey Davies*
Production Assistant: *Christine Lauricella*
Manufacturing Manager: *Ray Keating*
Art Director: *Merle Krumper*
Cover Coordinator: *Merle Krumper, Eric Dawson*
Illustrators: *Carlotta Tormey, Catherine Doyle Sullivan,*
    Shelly Matheis, Betsy Day, Matthew Daniel, Michelle LoGerfo
Realia: *Carey Davies, Michelle LoGerfo, Wendy Wolf*
Photo Research: *Vivian Garcia*
Interior Design: *Eric Dawson*
Cover Design: *Carmine Vecchio*

ISBN 0-13-908195-X

Reviewers: Robert A. Cote, *Lindsey Hopkins Technical Education Center;* Ulysses D'Aquila, *City College of San Francisco;* M. Sadiq Durrani, *BNC Santa Cruz;* Charles M. García, *University of Texas–Brownsville;* Kathleen Huggard Gómez, *Hunter College;* Kathy Hamilton, *Elk Grove Adult Education;* Kevin Keating, *University of Arizona;* Rosa Moreno, *Instituto Cultural Peruano–Norteamericano;* Betty Otiniano, *Instituto Cultural Peruano–Norteamericano;* Herbert D. Pierson, *St. John's University;* Alison M. Rice, *Hunter College;* Maria Rita Vieira, *Yazigi Language Schools, Brasil;* Tammy Smith-Firestone, *Edgewood Language Institute;* Garnet Templin-Imel, *Bellevue Community College*

Photo Credits: Prince Naruhito and Princess Masako of Japan, *Consulate General of Japan.* Hillary Rodham Clinton, *A/P World Photos.* Andy Garcia, *A/P World Photos.* Chinese New Year, *San Francisco Convention and Visitors Bureau.* Thai Festival of Lights, *Tourism Authority of Thailand, New York Office.* Fourth of July Celebration, *New York Convention & Visitors Bureau.* Spring and Summer, *Ray Keating.* Winter, *Peter Buckley.* Fall, *Michigan Department of Natural Resources.*

Contents

Pronunciation

Communication Skills

LISTENING AND SPEAKING

READING AND WRITING

Pronunciation	Listening and Speaking	Reading and Writing
• Falling intonation in greetings and leave-takings	• Introduce yourself and other people • Exchange information • Ask for and give a spelling • Listen for information	• Read for specific information • Make a class poster • Introduce oneself in writing
• Short /ɪ/ vs. long /i/	• Say and use numbers • Ask for the word in English of an object • Correct given information • Apologize	• Find information in phone and building directories • Make an address book
• Word stress	• Describe people • Listen for information • Get someone's attention • Ask someone to repeat	• Identify family members • Fill out a questionnaire • Write a paragraph
• Rising and falling intonation	• Ask about an apartment • Describe an apartment and the neighborhood • Describe locations	• Read real-estate ads • Write a simple ad • Write a description of one's neighborhood
• Word stress e.g., *thirteen* vs. *thirty*	• Ask and give the time • Talk about the weather and the seasons • Talk about on going actions • Talk about clothes and colors	• Read a weather map • Explain in writing one's opinion • Write a postcard
• Contrasting sounds: /t/ vs. /θ/	• Talk about daily routines • Talk about holidays	• Read for details • Write about daily routines • Write a short paragraph
• /a/ vs. /ə/, e.g., *cop* vs. *cup*	• Ask about availability • Ask for locations in a supermarket • Ask about prices • Discuss plans for a party	• Read advertisements • Follow directions in a recipe • Determine sequence in recipe instructions
• Questions with *or*	• Ask for information • Talk about likes/dislikes • Listen to recorded messages • Discuss use of leisure	• Read travel signs • Write a series of actions in proper sequence • Read entertainment schedules
• Rising intonation in *yes/no* questions	• Respond to interview questions • Talk about abilities • Discuss a person's suitability for a job	• Complete an application form • Create a Help Wanted ad • Read a performance review
• Final *-ed* sounds: /t/, /d/, /ɪd/	• Talk about past activities • Order in a restaurant • Make a suggestion, invite someone • Decline an invitation • Talk about future plans	• Read a menu • Create a personal time line

To the Teacher

New Vistas is a series that features the best of what has come to be known as "communicative language teaching," including recent developments in creating interactive, learner-centered curriculum. With *New Vistas,* your students become actively involved in their own language acquisition through collaboration with you as their guide and facilitator.

The Components of *New Vistas*

Student Books

The five-level student books begin with *Getting Started.* Here, students learn basic life skills and vocabulary. Then, in the subsequent levels, students develop their competence and proficiency step by step in all four skills.

Primary features of all the *Student Books* include a storyline with multi-ethnic characters, providing students with opportunities to be personally involved in real-life contexts for learning; a carefully graded series of pronunciation modules; many opportunities for group and pair interaction; listening comprehension exercises; a new and exciting online feature that introduces students to Internet technology; a strategy-awareness section in each unit that stimulates students to reflect on their own preferred pathways to success; and end-of-unit grammar and communication skills summaries.

Teacher's Resource Manuals

For each unit, the *Teacher's Resource Manual* provides an overview of topics, functions, communication skills, and skills standards covered. This is followed by step-by-step, explicit teaching instructions; answer keys for the exercises in the *Student Books* and the *Workbooks,* tapescripts for the listening and pronunciation exercises; grammar activity masters; and placement and achievement tests.

Workbooks

These supplements provide numerous written exercises that reinforce the grammar points and structures taught in the *Student Books. Workbook* exercises are suitable for additional in-class practice or for homework.

The Audio Programs

The audiotapes provide stimulating listening and pronunciation practice that add to the authenticity of classroom pedagogy.

Lesson 1

In this lesson, you will learn to

- introduce yourself.
- greet people and say good-bye.
- exchange personal information.
- ask how to spell something.

Hello. My name's Lynn.

Listen and read.

Lynn: Hello. My name's Lynn Wang.	**Yumiko:** It's nice to meet you.
Yumiko: Hi. I'm Yumiko Sato.	**Lynn:** Nice to meet you, too!
Lynn: Where are you from?	**Yumiko:** Is this your first visit here?
Yumiko: Tokyo. And you?	**Lynn:** Yes, I'm going to study English.
Lynn: I'm from Beijing.	

Pair Read the conversation with a partner.

Russia

ASIA

Yon Mi Lee
Pusan, Korea

Japan
South Korea

China

Taiwan

Philippines

Lynn Wang
Beijing, China

Yumiko Sato
Tokyo, Japan

North
Pacific
Ocean

NORTH
AMERICA

Ann Brennan
Houston, Texas
U.S.A.

United States

Mexico

Indian
Ocean

AUSTRALIA

South   Pacific   Ocean

New Zealand

1 Where is she from?

Look at the map. Then listen and repeat.

A: What's your name?
B: *Ann Brennan.*
A: Where are you from?
B: I'm from *Houston, Texas.*

A: What's her name?
B: Her name's *Gina Poggi.*
A: Where's she from?
B: She's from *Italy.*

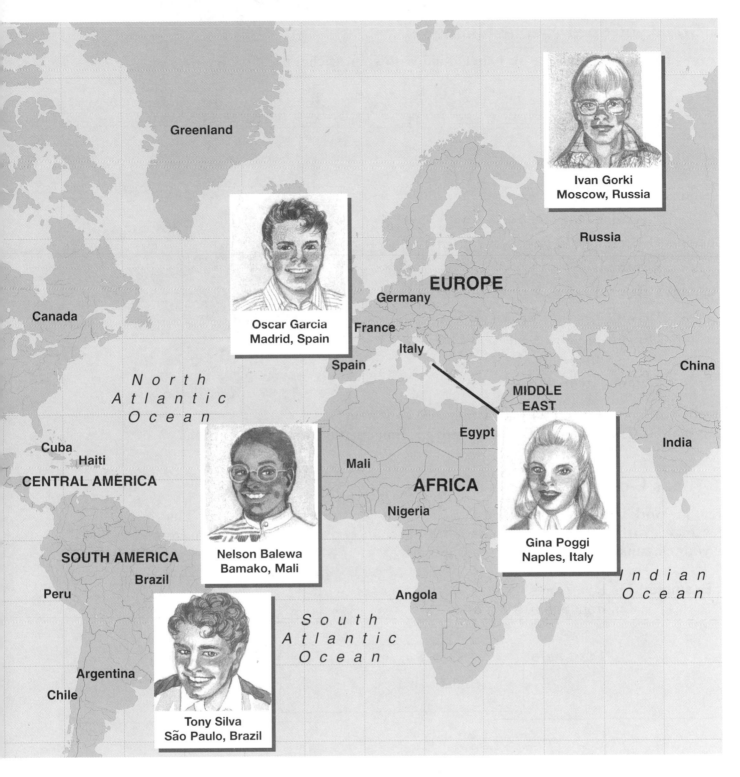

Pair Ask questions about the characters' names and places of origin.

A: Where is he from?   A: Where are you from?   A: Where is she from?
B: He's from Brazil.   B: I'm from Mexico.   B: She's from China.

Write your answers. What's your name? _____

Where are you from? _____

2 Could you spell your last name?

🔊 Listen. Then read the alphabet aloud with your teacher.

Aa   Bb   Cc   Dd   Ee   Ff   Gg   Hh   Ii   Jj   Kk   Ll   Mm
Nn   Oo   Pp   Qq   Rr   Ss   Tt   Uu   Vv   Ww   Xx   Yy   Zz

🔊 Listen and read.

Customs Officer: Name, please.

Gerard: *Gerard Davies.*

Customs Officer: Could you spell your last name?

Gerard: *D-a-v-i-e-s.*

Customs Officer: And your first name?

Gerard: *G-e-r-a-r-d.*

Customs Officer: Sign here, please. Welcome to the United States.

Gerard: Thank you.

Practice the conversation with a partner. Use your own information. Then listen to the other conversations that follow on the cassette.

3 That's L-o-l-a F-l-o-r-e-s.

Group Work in a group of six. Sit in a circle. Say your full name and spell it as your classmates write it in the seating chart. Say the country or city where you are from and spell it as your classmates write it in the seating chart.

Example: I'm Lola Flores. That's L-o-l-a F-l-o-r-e-s.
I'm from Spain. S-p-a-i-n.

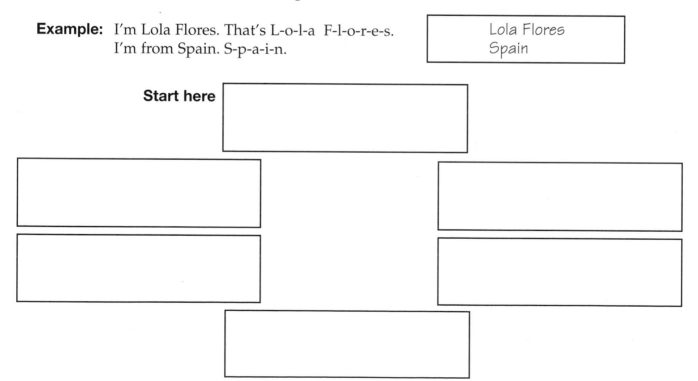

Lola Flores
Spain

Start here

Group Fill out the report below for your group.

1. Our group has _____ females.

2. Our group has _____ males.

3. Our group comes from _____ different countries/cities/towns.

4. Our group speaks _____ different languages.

Share the information about your group with the class.

Did you know that . . . ?
In the United States, when someone asks, "How are you?" or "How are you doing today?" a simple "Fine" or "I'm OK" is all he/she expects to hear.

4 Hear it. Say it.

Listen and read.

Falling Intonation

Good|MORN|ing.   Good|NIGHT.   See you|LA|ter.

Good|EVE|ning.   Good-|BYE.   Good after|NOON.

5 See you on Monday.

Listen and read.

Greetings		Leave-takings	
Hello.	Good afternoon.	Good-bye.	See you tomorrow.
Hi.	Good evening.	Bye.	See you later.
Good morning.		Good night.	See you on Monday.

Pair Fill in the blanks with a greeting or leave-taking. Then listen to the cassette and compare your answers. **Answers may vary.**

1. _Good morning_. How are you today?

2. _____, Ivan. Nice to meet you.

3. Good night, Oscar. See you _____.

4. _____. This is Channel 9's 11:00 o'clock news.

5. _____, Lynn. See you later.

At the end of class, say good-bye to your teacher and classmates.

Lesson 2

In this lesson, you will learn to
- introduce other people.
- exchange personal information.

Tony, this is Lynn.

🔊 Listen and read.

Yumiko: Hi, Tony. How are you?

Tony: Fine, thanks. And you?

Yumiko: Great! Tony, this is Lynn.
She's a new student. She's from China.

Tony: Nice to meet you, Lynn.

Lynn: Nice to meet you, too.

Group Work in groups of three. Introduce one member to the group.

Fine!
I'm doing well.

Not bad.

Not well.
Not too good.

1 He's Prince Naruhito, and she's Princess Masako.

🔊 **Listen and read.**

I am Ann Brennan.
You are Oscar Garcia.
He is Ivan Gorki.
She is Lynn Wang.
We are students.
They are Yumiko and Haro.

I'm from Houston.
You're from Madrid.
He's from Moscow.
She's from Beijing.
We're from Naples.
They're from Tokyo.

Subject Pronouns + *Be*	Contractions
I **am**	I**'m**
You **are**	You**'re**
He **is**	He**'s**
She **is**	She**'s**
We **are**	We**'re**
They **are**	They**'re**

Look at the photos. Complete the sentences below.

1. _____ Prince Naruhito and
   _____ Princess Masako.

   _____ from Japan.

2. _____ is Hillary Rodham Clinton.

   _____ from the United States.

3. He _____ Andy Garcia.

   _____ from Cuba.

Paste your photo here.

4. I _____ _____.

   _____ from _____.

Show the pictures to the class as you read the sentences aloud.

2 Find someone who . . .

Fill in each blank with a town, city, or country. Then find out who of your classmates come from this town, city, or country. Write your classmates' names in the second column.

Find someone in the class . . .	Name
1. who comes from _____	1. _____
2. who comes from _____	2. _____
3. who comes from _____	3. _____
4. who comes from _____	4. _____

Work in groups of ten. Complete the sentences below.

Example:

___Three___ students come from ___Jersey City___. His/Her/(Their) names is/(are)
___Alex Mercado, Ling Wei, and Olga Perchov_____.

1. _____ student(s) come(s) from _____. His/Her/Their name(s) is/are

   _____.

2. _____ student(s) come(s) from _____. His/Her/Their name(s) is/are

   _____.

3. _____ student(s) come(s) from _____. His/Her/Their name(s) is/are

   _____.

4. _____ student(s) come(s) from _____. His/Her/Their name(s) is/are

   _____.

Share the information with the class.

3 Information Gap Activity, pages 121 and 122.

Turn to pages 121 and 122. Follow your teacher's instructions.

Lesson 3

In this lesson, you will learn to
- read for specific information.
- write a brief report about a person.
- use the Internet.

This is our class.

Read about Mrs. Brennan and the students in her class.

This is Ann Brennan. She's from Houston, Texas. She's our English teacher.

Yumiko and Haro Sato are in English 1. They're from Tokyo.

Nelson Balewa is a new student. He's from Mali. He's in English 1, too.

Oscar Garcia is a new student, too. He's from Madrid, Spain.

This is Ivan Gorki. He's from Russia.

Here's Gina Poggi. She's from Italy.

Choose the correct answer.

1. His last name is Garcia.
   a. Ivan
   b. Nelson
   c. Oscar

2. She's a teacher.
   a. Ann
   b. Gina
   c. Yumiko

3. He's a new student.
   a. Ann
   b. Ivan
   c. Nelson

4. She's from Europe.
   a. Ann
   b. Nelson
   c. Gina

5. They speak Japanese.
   a. Ann and Gina
   b. Ivan and Oscar
   c. Yumiko and Haro

6. He is Russian.
   a. Ivan
   b. Oscar
   c. Nelson

Class Make a poster of your class with photos of all the students. Include their names and where they come from.

1 Online

Log onto **http://www.prenhall.com/brown_activities**
The Web: We're a world of nations.
Grammar: What's your grammar IQ?
E-mail: Hello, neighbor

2 Wrap Up

In the second column, write your responses.

What's your name?	
Where are you from?	
Where's he from? (*a male classmate*)	
Where's she from? (*a female classmate*)	
Where are your classmates from?	
Could you spell your last name?	
It's nice to meet you.	
See you tomorrow.	
How are you?	
Welcome to English 1.	

Mixer   After class discussion, your teacher will give you one question, statement, or answer to memorize. Find the person whose question, statement, or answer goes best with yours and move to the side of the classroom. The activity is finished when everybody finds a partner.

Pair   With your new partner, present your conversation to the class.

Strategies for Success

➤ **Writing things down on cards for easy review**
➤ **Reviewing your lessons with a partner**
➤ **Teaching to learn**

Look at the sentences in the **Communication Summary** on page 12.

1. Write the sentences on index cards or pieces of paper to carry with you.

2. In the next day or two, practice saying those sentences with a classmate. Make a dialog out of the sentences if possible. Keep saying the sentences to each other until you feel comfortable with them. Help your partner with difficult sounds.

3. Find a friend or colleague who doesn't know English. With your partner (or on your own), teach that person to say the sentences. You will be surprised at what you learn yourself!

CHECKPOINT ✔

I can	Yes!	Sometimes	Not Yet
introduce myself and other people.	❑	❑	❑
exchange personal information.	❑	❑	❑
greet people and say good-bye.	❑	❑	❑
ask someone to repeat.	❑	❑	❑
spell something and ask for spelling.	❑	❑	❑
ask and say where someone is from.	❑	❑	❑

Learning Preferences

Think about the work you did in this unit. Put a check next to the items that helped you learn the lessons. Put two checks next to the ones that helped a lot.

❑ ❑ Listening to the teacher
❑ ❑ Working by myself
❑ ❑ Working with a partner
❑ ❑ Working with a group
❑ ❑ Asking the teacher questions

❑ ❑ Listening to the tapes and doing exercises
❑ ❑ Writing paragraphs
❑ ❑ Reading
❑ ❑ Using the Internet

VOCABULARY

Things and People		Action Words
city	name	come
classmate	news	listen
country	student	meet
customs officer	teacher	sign
female	town	spell
language	visit	study
male		

▶ GRAMMAR SUMMARY

SIMPLE PRESENT TENSE

Subject Pronoun	
Singular	**Plural**
I	we
you	you
he	
she }	they
it	

Subject Pronoun or Noun	*Be*	
I	am	
He She It	is	from China.
We They	are	
My name	's	Ivan.

Subject +*Be*	Contractions
I **am**	I**'m**
You **are**	You**'re**
He **is**	He**'s**
She **is**	She**'s**
It **is**	It**'s**
We **are**	We**'re**
They **are**	They**'re**

Question Word	*Be*	Subject Pronoun or Noun	
Where	is	he she it	from?
	are	you they	
What	's	your name?	

▶ COMMUNICATION SUMMARY

Greeting people
Hi. *or* Hello. How are you?
Good morning/afternoon/evening/night.

Introducing yourself
My name's Ivan.
I'm Oscar.

Introducing others
Lynn, this is Yumiko.
　(It's) Nice to meet you.

Asking how to spell something
Could you spell your last name?

Exchanging personal information
What's your name?
　My name's Ivan Gorki.
Where are you from?
　I'm from Russia.
What class are you in?
　I'm in English 1.

Saying good-bye
Good-bye. *or* Bye.
　See you tomorrow./See you later.

Thanking
Thank you. *or* Thanks.

UNIT 2

Lesson 1

In this lesson, you will learn to
- say and use numbers.
- ask for and give addresses and phone numbers.
- ask someone to repeat.
- correct given information.
- thank a person and accept thanks.

What's your address?

Lynn is getting a library card. Listen and read.

Librarian: What's your name, please?

Lynn: Lynn Wang.

Librarian: What's your address?

Lynn: 6363 Richmond Street.

Librarian: And your phone number?

Lynn: Excuse me?

Librarian: What's your telephone number?

Lynn: 555-4310.

Pair Practice with a partner. Use your own information.

1 Word Bag: Numbers

 Listen and read.

0 zero/oh	1 one	2 two	3 three	4 four	5 five
6 six	7 seven	8 eight	9 nine	10 ten	11 eleven
12 twelve	13 thirteen	14 fourteen	15 fifteen	16 sixteen	17 seventeen
18 eighteen	19 nineteen	20 twenty	21 twenty-one	22 twenty-two	30 thirty
40 forty	50 fifty	60 sixty	70 seventy	80 eighty	90 ninety
100 one hundred	1,000 one thousand				

2 Addresses and Phone Numbers

 Listen and read.

Did you know that . . . ? In the U.S., you have to use zip codes on letter envelopes and packages for delivery.

Area Code and Telephone Numbers

1. (401) 555–8022
2. (803) 555–4321

Zip Codes

3. 10023
4. 94118

Course Numbers

5. English 101
6. Math 2

Room Numbers

7. Room 304
8. Room 1011

Addresses

9. 709 Elm Street
10. 6215 University Street

Years

11. 1900
12. 1998

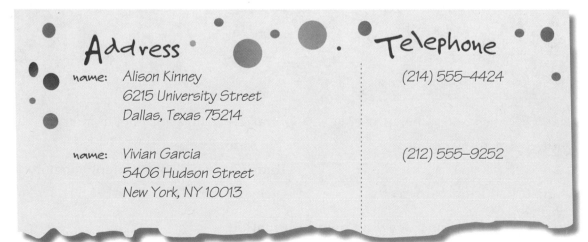

Address

name: Alison Kinney
6215 University Street
Dallas, Texas 75214

Telephone

(214) 555–4424

name: Vivian Garcia
5406 Hudson Street
New York, NY 10013

(212) 555–9252

3 Don't mention it.

Look at the picture. Listen and read.

Librarian: Here's a temporary library card.
Please check the information.

Lynn: [*pause*] Excuse me. The phone number
here is wrong. It's not 555-4301.
My correct number is 555-4310.

Librarian: Oh, I'm sorry. Let me correct that.

Lynn: Thank you.

Librarian: You're welcome.

Practice the conversation with a partner. Use the information in the ID cards and the expressions below. Each ID card has one wrong number. Correct the number.

Thanking	Responding to Thanks
Thank you.	You're welcome.
Thank you very much.	That's all right.
Thanks a lot.	That's OK.
Thanks very much.	Don't mention it.
Thanks a million!	My pleasure!

Employee Information Card

Name:
Aiko Mizoi

Social Security Number:
431-88-6431

Phone Number:
(415) 555-201~~2~~
            3

New York State

Driver's License

John Anderson
3294 Park Avenue
New York, NY 10001
                 7
Date of Birth: May ~~9~~, 1970

4 Is that in the city?

Listen to the librarian talk
to three people. Complete the chart.

Name	Street	Telephone
Anna Jones	124 Main Street	
Ali Al-Khati		555-9321
	39 Richmond Avenue	

5 Concentration Game, page 123.

Cut out the cards on page 123. Shuffle the number cards. Place them, face down, on the table. Do the same for the word cards. Take turns turning over a word card and a number card. If the two match, read the word and keep the cards. If the cards don't match, put back the cards, face down. The student with the most pairs of matching cards wins.

Lesson 2

In this lesson, you will learn to
- identify classroom objects.
- understand classroom commands and perform the actions.
- confirm or correct information.

Is this Room 102?

Lynn is looking for her English class. Listen and read.

Mr. Miller: Hi. Are you a new student?

Lynn: Yes, I am. Am I late for class?

Mr. Miller: No, you aren't. You're early.

Lynn: Is this Room 102?

Mr. Miller: No, it isn't. It's Room 202.

Lynn: Oh. Is this English 1?

Mr. Miller: No, it isn't. It's Math 1.

Lynn: Oh, excuse me. I'm in the wrong room.

Listen and read again. Check (✓) *True* or *False* after each sentence.

	True	False
1. Lynn is late for class.	_____	_____
2. Lynn is in Room 102.	_____	_____
3. Lynn is lost.	_____	_____
4. Mr. Miller is in Room 202.	_____	_____
5. Lynn is in the right room.	_____	_____

1 Word Bag: The Classroom

Look at the pictures of classroom objects and read the labels for each.

Pair With a partner, ask and answer questions about the items in the picture.

Examples:

A: What's *this*?
B: It's *a pencil*.

A: What's *that*?
B: It's *an eraser*.

Go around your classroom with your partner. Make a list of other items in the room that you can name. Share your list with the class.

Now look at the pictures below and read the label under each.

1. Turn on the light.

2. Turn off the projector.

3. Take notes in your notebook.

4. Open your book.

5. Close your book.

6. Hand in your homework.

7. Stand up.

8. Sit down.

9. Erase the board.

Your teacher will tell someone in your class to perform the action in one of the pictures above. Then it is your turn to call on a different student. Continue in this way until everyone in class has had a turn to perform an action.

2 Hear it. Say it.

Listen to each pair of words. Is the vowel sound the same or different?
Circle *same* or *different*.

Sounds /ɪ/ in *this* and /i/ in *these*

1.	same	different	5.	same	different
2.	same	different	6.	same	different
3.	same	different	7.	same	different
4.	same	different	8.	same	different

3 What's the word in English?

Pair   Ask and answer questions about things in your classroom. Use the expressions below. If you don't understand what your partner says, ask him or her to say it again.

A: How do you say *this/that* in English?
B: This/that is a *computer*.
A: I'm sorry. I didn't hear what you said.
B: I said, "This/that is a *computer*."

A: What's the English word for *this/that*?
B: It's *calculator*.
A: Can you repeat that, please?
B: I said, "It's *calculator*."

A: What do you call *this/that* in English?
B: It's called a *pencil sharpener*.
A: What do you call it? A *pen sharpener*?
B: No. It's a *pencil sharpener*.

T: Class, turn on your monitors.
A: What does *monitor* mean?
B: The *monitor* is the television part of the computer.
A: Sorry, I don't understand. Can you say that again?
B: Yes, the *monitor* is the television part of the computer.

4 Classroom Directory

🔊 Look at the directory and listen to the conversation.

A: Where's *English 2*?
B: It's in *Room 222*.

A: Is *English 3* in *Room 322*?
B: No, it isn't. It's in *Room 324*.

**World English Center
Classroom Directory**

	Room
English 1	102
Registrar's Office	122
Gym	125
Cafeteria	126
English 2	222
Counselor's Office	223
English 3	324
Library	325
English 4	416

Pair Ask and answer questions. Follow the examples. Then work with your partner to make a Classroom Directory for your school. Present your directory to the class.

5 Are you in English 1?

🔊 Listen and read.

A: **Are you** in English 1?
B: Yes, **I am**. *or* No, **I'm not**.
A: **Is he/she** a new student?
B: Yes, **he/she is**. *or* No, **he/she isn't**.

A: **Are your classmates** all here?
B: Yes, **they are**. *or* No, **they aren't**.

Pair Ask and answer the questions. Follow the examples.

1. Are you in this class? _____

2. Are all the students in class today? _____

3. Is this Room 101? _____

4. Is your teacher from New York? _____

5. Is he/she a good teacher? _____

In this lesson, you will learn to

- understand symbols and instructions on a public telephone.
- read for specific information.

Let's use the public telephone.

Look at the picture of a public phone. Read the instructions on the phone.

5¢ • 10¢ • 25¢
1 Listen for Tone
2 Deposit Coins
3 Dial Number

COIN RELEASE

Area Code (713) 555-6831

1	ABC 2	DEF 3
GHI 4	JKL 5	MNO 6
PRS 7	TUV 8	WXY 9
*	OPER 0	#

DIALING INSTRUCTIONS

COIN CALLS
Local Calls.......................... Deposit Coins then Dial the Number
Long Distance.................... Dial **1** + Area Code + the Number
NO COIN NEEDED TO DIAL
EMERGENCIES
Police, Fire, Ambulance... 911
Other Emergencies... **0** (Operator)

CREDIT CARD – COLLECT – PERSON-TO-PERSON
Dial **0** + Area Code + the Number

DIRECTORY ASSISTANCE
713 Area.. 555-1212
Other Areas........................... **1** + Area Code + 555-1212

PUSH FOR COIN

Pair Tell your partner how to use a pay phone. Write the steps below.

_____

_____

_____

Did you know that . . . ?
In the U.S., 911 is the number to call for all kinds of emergencies. It is the number to call if you need the police or the fire department, or if you need to rush someone to a hospital.

1 What number can you call?

Pair Work with a partner. Answer the following questions.

1. To make a long-distance call, what do you dial first? _____

2. You want to report a fire. What number can you call? _____

3. You need to call a hospital. You know the hospital's name and location, but you don't know the phone number. What do you dial to get the hospital's phone number? _____

4. You want to call 1-800-DENTIST. What numbers do you dial? _____

2 Online

Log onto **http://www.prenhall.com/brown_activities**
The Web: Let's explore the languages of the world.
Grammar: What's your grammar IQ?
E-mail: Long–distance "Hello"

3 Wrap Up

Group Make a Class Directory on a page of your English notebook. Ask eight classmates their names, addresses, and telephone numbers, and write the information in your directory.

What's your name?
What's your address?
What's your phone number?

Class Directory		
Name	Address	Telephone number

Strategies for Success

➤ **Interviewing**
➤ **Recording your information**
➤ **Practicing with a partner**

1. In this unit, you made a directory of addresses and phone numbers of people in your class. Find at least ten other people in your school or at work who are also taking English classes. In English, ask for their addresses and phone numbers.

2. Record the information in your directory.

3. Practice your information with your partner like this:
    Jose Garcia lives at 2213 Ygnacio Street in Los Angeles, California.
    His phone number is 555-9853.

CHECKPOINT

I can	Yes!	Sometimes	Not Yet
ask someone to repeat.	☐	☐	☐
confirm and correct information.	☐	☐	☐
apologize, give thanks/accept thanks.	☐	☐	☐
say and use numbers.	☐	☐	☐
ask for/give addresses/phone numbers.	☐	☐	☐
identify objects in the classroom.	☐	☐	☐
understand and perform commands.	☐	☐	☐
understand signs on a public telephone.	☐	☐	☐

Learning Preferences

Think about the work you did in this unit. Put a check next to the items that helped you learn the lessons. Put two checks next to the ones that helped a lot.

☐ ☐ Listening to the teacher   ☐ ☐ Listening to the tapes and doing the exercises
☐ ☐ Working by myself   ☐ ☐ Reading
☐ ☐ Working with a partner   ☐ ☐ Writing paragraphs
☐ ☐ Working with a group   ☐ ☐ Using the Internet
☐ ☐ Asking the teacher questions

VOCABULARY

Classroom Items/Words

book	keyboard
bookshelf	light
chair	monitor
chalkboard	notebook
clock	pen
computer	pencil
desk	pencil sharpener
dictionary	piece of chalk
door	printer
eraser	projector
file cabinet	window
globe	

Phone Use

coin
deposit
dial
emergency
fire
hospital
local call
long distance
police

Addresses and Phone Numbers

address
area code
avenue
phone number
street
zip code

▶ GRAMMAR SUMMARY

Indefinite Articles (*a, an*)
That's **a** pen.
That's **an** eraser.

Affirmative Statements
It's a pen.
They're chairs.
She's Mrs. Brennan.

Singular Nouns
a pen
an eraser

Plural Nouns
pen**s**
eraser**s**

Yes/No Questions	Short Answers
Am I in the right class?	Yes, you **are**. No, you **aren't**.
Are you the teacher?	Yes, I **am**. No, I'**m not**.
Is he/she the teacher?	Yes, he/she **is**. No, he/she **isn't**.

▶ COMMUNICATION SUMMARY

Exchanging personal information
Are you a new student?
    Yes, I am. *or* No, I'm not.
What's your name?
    Lynn Wang.
What's your address?
    6363 Richmond Street.
What's your telephone number?
    555-4310.

Confirming and correcting information
Am I late for class?
    Yes, you are. *or* No, you aren't.
Is this Room 222?
Is this English 2?
    Yes, it is. *or* No, it isn't. It's English 1.

Thanking and accepting thanks
Thank you.
    You're welcome.

Apologizing
Excuse me. I'm in the wrong room.

Asking someone to repeat
Excuse me?

Asking about and identifying objects
What's this/that?
    It's a book.
What's that?
    It's an eraser.

UNIT 3

Lesson 1

In this lesson, you will learn to
- identify family members.
- exchange personal information.

That baby is really cute!

Look at the picture. Listen and read.

Lynn: Is this your family?

Oscar: Yes, it is. These are my parents, and this is my sister Alicia.

Lynn: She's pretty. Is she married?

Oscar: Yes, she is. This is her husband, Felix, and these are her children, Pedro and Jacinta.

Lynn: That baby is really cute! Is this another sister?

Oscar: Yes. Her name's Stella.

Lynn: Is she married?

Oscar: No, she isn't. She's a student.

Lynn: Are the boy and girl between you and Stella also your brother and sister?

Oscar: Yes, my little brother, Bobby, and my sister Maria.

Lynn: What a big beautiful family!

Pair Read the above conversation with a partner.

Circle *True*, *False*, or *Don't Know*.

1.	Alicia is married.	True	False	Don't know
2.	Felix has children.	True	False	Don't know
3.	Oscar has sisters and a brother.	True	False	Don't know
4.	Alicia is Felix's wife.	True	False	Don't know
5.	Lynn has a brother.	True	False	Don't know

1 Word Bag: The Family

Look at the picture. Listen and repeat. Then answer this question: How is each person related to Oscar? Write the family word on the line after each person's name. Use each word once. You can put two words on one line if appropriate.

grandfather	grandmother	father	mother	daughter	brother	nephew
husband	sister	wife	son	aunt	uncle	niece

Mr. Garcia _____

Mrs. Garcia _____

Alicia _____

Felix _____
Oscar's brother-in-law

Pedro _____

Jacinta _____

Oscar _____
Pedro's uncle

Stella _____

Bobby _____

Maria _____

Pair Compare your answers with a partner. Now, answer this question: How is each person related to Pedro? Write your answer below each name.

Did you know that . . . ?
In the U.S., grandparents rarely live with their married sons or daughters. Grandparents usually live on their own.

2 Is Alicia Oscar's sister?

Pair Look at Oscar's family above. Ask and answer questions. Follow the examples below.

A: **Is** Alicia Oscar's sister?
B: Yes, **she is.**
A: **Is** Pedro Stella's brother?
B: No, **he isn't.**

A: **Are** Oscar and Bobby brothers?
B: Yes, **they are.**
A: **Are** Felix and Oscar brothers?
B: No, **they aren't.**

3 Our last name is Gorki.

🔊 **Listen and read. Then fill in the blanks with** *my, his, her, its, our,* **and** *their.*

My name is Sofia. This is my husband. **His** name is Vladimir. This is my daughter. **Her** name is Sonia.

These are my sons. **Their** names are Ivan and Vanya. **Our** last name is Gorki. This is my dog. **Its** name is Tex.

1. Hello. _____ name is Sofia.

2. And this is my husband. _____ name is Vladimir.

3. This is my daughter. _____ name is Sonia.

4. These are my sons. _____ names are Ivan and Vanya. _____ last name is Gorki.

5. This is our dog. _____ name is Tex.

4 Hear it. Say it.

🔊 **Listen and read.**

Word Stress

1. móther
2. fáther
3. bróther
4. síster

5. úncle
6. coúsin
7. grándfàther
8. gràndmóther

5 Here's my family.

Use pictures of your family members or write their names in the family tree. Add circles if you need to. Then fill in the blanks with *my, his, her, its, our,* or *their.*

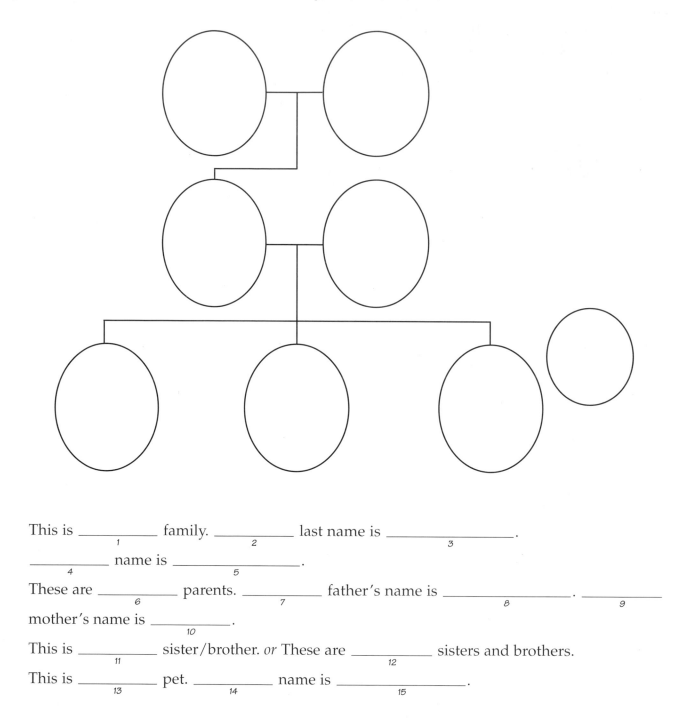

This is _____ family. _____ last name is _____.
         1   2   3

_____ name is _____.
4   5

These are _____ parents. _____ father's name is _____. _____
          6   7   8   9

mother's name is _____.
                 10

This is _____ sister/brother. *or* These are _____ sisters and brothers.
        11   12

This is _____ pet. _____ name is _____.
        13   14   15

6 Relative Name Tag Game, page 124.

Group Turn to page 124. Your teacher will place a relationship name tag on your back. (You can't look at it.) Show your name tag to members of your group. Ask each classmate one question to find out your relationship to Mrs. Solo. When you think you know what relative you are, write your name on Mrs. Solo's family tree. Then look at the tag on your back.

7 Are you an only child?

Fill out the questionnaire below about yourself and your family.

Examples:

A: Are you married?
B: *Yes, I am.* or *No, I'm not.*
A: Do you have brothers and sisters?
B: *Yes, I do.* or *No, I don't.*

A: How many brothers do you have?
B: *I have one brother.*
A: How many sisters do you have?
B: *I have two sisters.*

For older students

Are you married?

_____

Do you have any sisters?

_____

How many?

_____

Do you have any brothers?

_____

How many?

_____

Do you have any sons?

_____

How many?

_____

Do you have any daughters?

_____

How many?

_____

For younger students

Are you an only child?

_____

Do you have any sisters and brothers?

_____

How many sisters do you have?

_____

How many brothers do you have?

_____

How many children do your parents
have? _____

Is your sister/brother married?

_____

Does she/he have children?

_____

Group In groups of five, have one member interview the others with the questionnaire above. He/she writes the information about your group. Share your information with your classmates.

_____ has the most sisters or daughters.

_____ has the most brothers or sons.

_____ of our group members have no brothers or sisters.

Lesson 2

In this lesson, you will learn to

- exchange information about the family.
- write about the family.

I have an interesting family.

🔊 Listen and read.

I have an interesting family. This is my father, Leonardo. He's a famous Italian actor. That's my mother, Elizabeth. She's a doctor. Over here is Uncle Luigi. He is the chef in his own Italian restaurant. He makes fabulous pasta!

This is my favorite cousin, Vito. He's a waiter in his father's restaurant. He goes to college at night. That's his sister, Stephanie. She's an engineer. She's the only woman at her construction site.

I'm an English student. I want to teach English someday.

Read the above paragraphs aloud. Match the person with the occupation. Write the letter in the blank.

_____ 1. Luigi Poggi   _____ 4. Gina Poggi   a. waiter   d. student

_____ 2. Leonardo Poggi   _____ 5. Vito Poggi   b. doctor   e. actor

_____ 3. Stephanie Poggi   _____ 6. Elizabeth Poggi   c. chef   f. engineer

1 This is my uncle Luigi.

Class Bring photos of an interesting member of your family to class. Go around the room. Ask and answer questions about the family photos.

Examples:

A: Who is this?

B: That's my uncle.

A: What's his name?

B: His name is Luigi.

A: How old is he?

B: He's 40 years old.

A: Where does he live?

B: He lives in Italy.

2 We're in show business.

Pair Fill in the blanks with *am, is, are, have,* or *has.*

Everyone in my family _____ in the entertainment business. My grandmother _____ a job on TV. She is a singer. My grandfather _____ a musician. He works for a radio station. My aunt _____ an actress, and my uncle _____ a writer. My uncle _____ important in Hollywood. I _____ an actor. We all _____ interesting jobs. We _____ happy to be in show business. It _____ an exciting field.

Write a short paragraph. Tell something interesting about your family. Then share your story with your classmates.

_____

_____

_____

_____

_____

_____

_____

_____

_____

Singular Subject	Verb
I You	have
He She It	has
Plural Subject	Verb
We You They	have

Lesson 3

In this lesson, you will learn to
- read for specific information.
- ask for a description of a person.
- describe people.
- express interest.

The Cheshire Family

🔲 **Listen and read.**

The Cheshire family is a typical cat-loving family. They live at 9 Feline Street in Cougarville. The father's name is Leo Cheshire, and the mother's name is Felicia. Tiger is their son, and Kitty is their daughter. The cats are members of the family, too.

Leo is short and has brown hair. His cat, Racer, has brown hair, too. Felicia is a large woman. She has blond hair. Her cat, Honey, is also blond. Kitty and her cat, Einstein, both have dark hair and dark eyes. Kitty's hair is straight, and she wears glasses, but Einstein doesn't. His eyes are very good. Kitty's brother, Tiger, and his big, strong cat named Gus both have red hair and blue eyes. "Gus is always hungry," says Tiger, "just like me!"

Pair Put a check (✓) before the correct answer.

1.	The Cheshire family loves	_____ cats.	_____ dogs.
2.	Leo Cheshire is Tiger's	_____ father.	_____ uncle.
3.	Felicia is Kitty's	_____ aunt.	_____ mother.
4.	Kitty is Tiger's	_____ cousin.	_____ sister.
5.	Tiger's eyes are	_____ blue.	_____ brown.
6.	Kitty and Einstein have	_____ dark hair.	_____ curly hair.
7.	Gus is	_____ strong.	_____ elegant.
8.	Leo is	_____ tall.	_____ short.
9.	Felicia's hair is	_____ blond.	_____ black.
10.	The Cheshires look like	_____ each other.	_____ their cats.

Class Do you know anyone who looks like his/her pet? Tell the class about him/her.

32 UNIT 3

1 Physical Characteristics

Look at the pictures. Listen and read.

Height

short   average   tall   thin   average   heavy

Weight

Hair/Eyes

long blond/light blue   short black/dark brown   straight brown/black

curly red/green   bald head/hazel

2 Let's play Twenty Questions.

Class   Think of a classmate. Your classmates will take turns to guess the person you have picked. They can ask 20 questions, such as "Is this person a man or a woman?" "Is he/she short or tall?" "Does he/she have brown hair?" The person who guesses the name thinks of another classmate. In your notebook, write a description of the person you selected.

3 Online:

Log onto **http://www.prenhall.com/brown_activities**
The Web: Let's keep in touch.
Grammar: What's your grammar IQ?
E-mail: My family

4 Wrap Up

Pair   Interview your partner and write his/her description. Indent each paragraph. Write your paragraphs in your notebook.

I'm in the News

Paragraph 1

1. What's your name?

2. What's your nationality?

3. What city and country are you from?

4. Are you tall, short, or average height?

5. Describe your hair and your eyes.

6. What do you do?

Paragraph 2

1. Are you married? (For older students)

2. Do you have any children? (For older students)

3. Do you have brothers and sisters? How many?

4. Are you and your family in the United States now?

5. Where do you live right now?

Strategies for Success

➤ **Keeping a journal**
➤ **Using words in a new context**

Get a small notebook to use for the whole course. It will be your personal journal. In this unit, you made a family tree.

1. For your first entry, write short descriptions of each member of your family. Use the vocabulary and sentences you have learned. Remember to describe who they are (sister, mother, etc.), their ages, physical characteristics, and occupations, if any.

2. Write a description of yourself.

3. Write a description of your teacher.

CHECKPOINT ✔

I can	Yes!	Sometimes	Not Yet
identify and talk about family members.	❑	❑	❑
exchange personal information.	❑	❑	❑
get someone's attention.	❑	❑	❑
ask someone to repeat.	❑	❑	❑
ask about and describe a person.	❑	❑	❑
express interest.	❑	❑	❑

Learning Preferences

Think about the work you did in this unit. Put a check next to the items that helped you learn the lessons. Put two checks next to the ones that helped a lot.

❑ ❑ Listening to the teacher
❑ ❑ Working by myself
❑ ❑ Working with a partner
❑ ❑ Working with a group
❑ ❑ Asking the teacher questions

❑ ❑ Listening to the tapes and doing exercises
❑ ❑ Reading
❑ ❑ Writing paragraphs
❑ ❑ Using the Internet

VOCABULARY

Family Members	Physical Characteristics	Marital Status	Occupations
brother, sister	average height	married	actor
child (children)	average weight	single	architect
cousin	bald		chef
father, mother	beautiful		construction worker
grandchildren	black/blond/brown/red hair		doctor
grandfather	blue/brown/gray/green/hazel		engineer
grandmother	eyes		musician
husband, wife	cute		singer
nephew	curly/straight		student
niece	heavy		waiter
parents	light/dark		writer
son, daughter	long/short hair		
uncle, aunt	pretty		
	short		
	tall		
	thin		

Possessive Adjectives
What's **your** name? **My** name's Sofia.
His name's Vladimir. **Her** name's Sonia.
Its name's Tex. **Our** last name is Gorki.
Their names are Ivan and Vanya.

Possessive 's
This is **Gina's** father.
What's **Oscar's** occupation?

Information (Wh-) Questions
Who's that?
    That's Luigi Poggi.
What is his occupation?
    He's a chef.
How old is he?
    He's 40 years old.

Adjectives
Leo is **short** and **bald**.
Einstein has **dark** hair.

Negative Statements

I	'm not	
He She	isn't	in France now.
We You They	aren't	

Present Tense: Has/Have

Subject	Verb	Object
I	have	
He She It	has	green eyes.
We You They	have	

► COMMUNICATION SUMMARY

Identifying people
Who's that?
    That's Gina Poggi.
Is that your father?
    Yes, it is. *or* No, it isn't.
This is my brother.
    His name is Felix.

Describing people
Roger is average height.
He has brown hair and green eyes.

Exchanging personal information
What's your occupation?
    I'm a teacher.
How old are you?
    I'm 35.
Are you married?
    Yes, I am. *or* No, I'm not.
Do you have any children?
    No, I haven't. *or*
    Yes. I have a son.

Getting someone's attention
Excuse me.

Asking someone to repeat
Excuse me?
What?

Lesson 1

In this lesson, you will learn to
- ask about an apartment.
- describe an apartment.
- describe differences.
- ask for and give locations.

I'm calling about the apartment on Summer Street.

 Listen and read.

Lynn: Hello. I'm calling about the apartment on Summer Street. How many rooms are there?

Realtor: There are two bedrooms, a living room, a large kitchen, and a bathroom.

Lynn: Are there big closets?

Realtor: Yes, there are. There are two large closets in the bedrooms.

Lynn: Is there a dishwasher?

Realtor: No, there isn't.

Lynn: When can I see the apartment?

Realtor: How about tomorrow at 10:00?

Read the conversation again. Circle *True*, *False*, or *Don't know*.

1.	There are two bedrooms in the apartment.	True	False	Don't know
2.	There's a TV in the living room.	True	False	Don't know
3.	There's a dishwasher in the kitchen.	True	False	Don't know
4.	There are five rooms in the apartment.	True	False	Don't know
5.	There's a closet near the main door.	True	False	Don't know

1 Word Bag: Household Items

Look at the picture. Listen and repeat.

2 The stove is in the kitchen.

Pair Look at the picture above. Write the names of the objects in the rooms where they belong. Some items can be used in more than one room.

living room	kitchen	dining room	bathroom	bedroom	closet

Add three more words to each list.

3 Place Lynn's furniture in her living room.

 **Look at the drawings. Listen and read.**

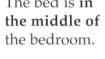 There's a sofa **between** two end tables.

between

The pictures are **on** the wall.

on

 The bed is **in the middle of** the bedroom.

in the middle of

 The sofa is **in the corner of** the living room.

in the corner of

under

The cat is **under** the chair.

 The armchair is **next to** the sofa.

next to

 There's a cat **in front of** the sofa.

in front of

Study the symbols and the floor plan.

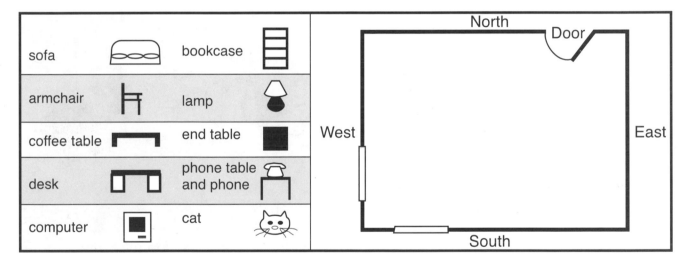

sofa		bookcase	
armchair		lamp	
coffee table		end table	
desk		phone table and phone	
computer		cat	

Pair Place Lynn's furniture in her living room. Use the symbols above.

1. There's a sofa **in the middle of** the east wall **between** two end tables.

2. There's a coffee table **in front of** the sofa.

3. There's a phone **on** the table **in the corner of** the north and west walls.

4. There's a desk on the west wall **between** the window and the north wall.

5. There's a computer **on** the desk.

6. There are two bookcases on the south wall **between** the window and the east wall.

7. There is a cat **under** the phone table.

8. The lamp is **next to** the south window.

4 There are pictures on the walls.

Pair Look at the floor plan on page 39 and take turns describing it.

Examples: There's a coffee table in front of the sofa.
There are pictures on the wall.

Look around your classroom. On a piece of paper, write sentences describing the locations of five objects in your classroom.

5 Hear it. Say it.

Listen and repeat.

Rising and Falling Intonation

1. There's a so|fa in the living room.

2. There isn't a| ba|by in the picture.

3. Is there a| lamp on the table?

4. Is there a| phone in the kitchen?

5. There aren't any| flo|wers on the table.

6. Are there any| lamps in the room?

6 There aren't any pictures on the walls.

Pair Are the pictures the same or different? Say what is different about them.

Picture A **Picture B**

Examples: There isn't a television in Picture A.
There aren't any pictures on the wall in Picture B.

1. rug under the table

2. a bookcase next to the window

3. curtains on the windows

4. picture above the table

5. lamp in the room

6. a coffee table on the rug

7 Are there public phones in this school?

Look around your school and ask five *yes/no* questions.

Examples:

A: Is there a Women's Room on this floor?
B: Yes, there is. *or* No, there isn't.

A: Are there public phones in this school?
B: Yes, there are. *or* No, there aren't.

Lesson 2

In this lesson, you will learn to
- ask for a description of a neighborhood.
- describe a neighborhood.
- ask for locations.
- give locations.

Lynn's new address is 317 Elm Street.

Look at the picture. Listen and read.

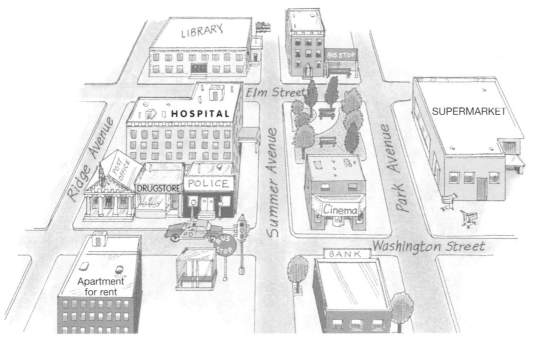

Dear Mom and Dad,

Yumiko and I are finally in our new apartment. It's on Elm Street in a nice neighborhood. The bus stop is right next to our building. There's a park across from our building. We can walk across the street and enjoy the trees and flowers.

*There is a supermarket, a drugstore, a post office, a bank, a movie theater, and a police station near our apartment building. The post office is on the corner of Ridge Avenue and Washington Street. The drugstore is between the post office and the police station. There is a library and a hospital in our neighborhood, too.

Our new address is 317 Elm Street. We hope you can come and visit us soon.

Love,

Lynn

*"There is" followed by a series of singular nouns is acceptable in oral conversation and informal communication.

1 The apartment is across from a park.

🔊 Look at the buildings on page 41. Listen and repeat. Then match the words and the pictures.

_____ bank	_____ drugstore	_____ police station
_____ supermarket	_____ bus stop	_____ movie theater
_____ hospital	_____ apartment building	_____ library

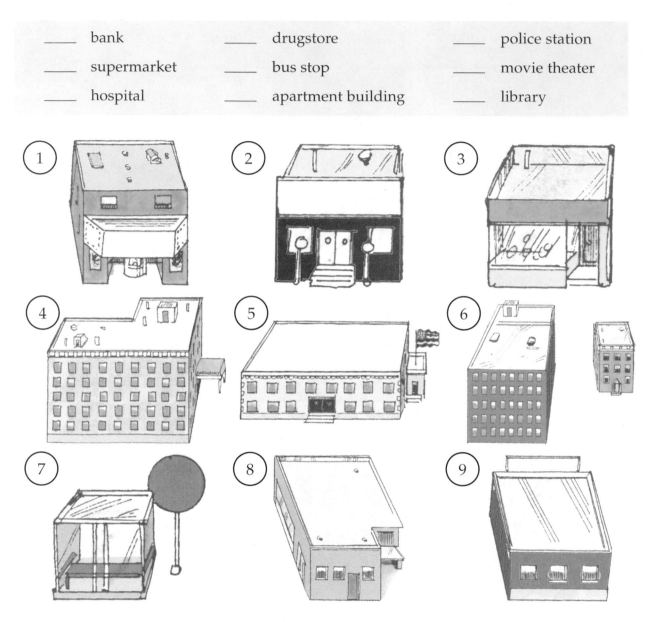

2 It's in a very nice neighborhood.

Read the letter on page 41. Fill in the blanks.

Did you know that . . . ?
In the U.S., the highest cost of housing is in New York City, Los Angeles, and Washington.

1. The apartment is _____ Elm Street.

2. There is a park _____ from our apartment.

3. There is a bus stop _____ to the apartment building.

4. There is a post office _____ of Washington Street and Ridge Avenue.

5. There is a supermarket _____ our apartment.

3 There's a drugstore on Washington Street.

Listen as you look at the map.

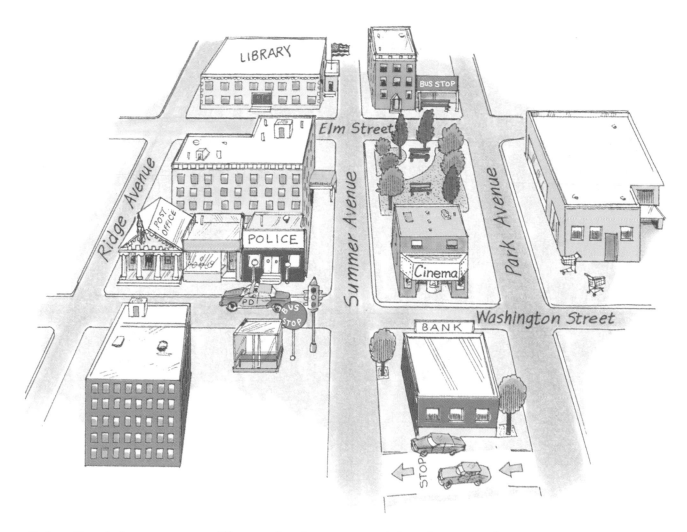

Pair Read the sentences. Then write the names of the places on the map.

1. Lynn and Yumiko have a new apartment. Their **apartment building** is on Elm Street. It's across from a park.

2. There's a **drugstore** on Washington Street. It's between the post office and the police station.

3. The **movie theater** is on Washington Street. It's across from the bank.

4. There's a **supermarket** on Park Avenue. It's between Elm Street and Washington Street.

5. There's a **hospital** on the corner of Ridge Avenue and Elm Street. It's across from the library.

6. There's a **park** on Elm Street. It's between Summer Avenue and Park Avenue.

4 Information Gap Activity, pages 125 and 126.

Pair Turn to pages 125 and 126. Follow your teacher's instructions.

5 Excuse me. Where's the library?

Pair   Look at the map on page 43. Ask and answer questions.

Example:

A: Excuse me. Where's *the library*?
B: It's *on the corner of Elm Street and Summer Avenue.* (It's *across from the hospital.*)
A: Thank you.

6 I live in a quiet neighborhood.

Write a description of your neighborhood. You may use the questions below for ideas. Use *across from, next to, near,* **and** *between* **where needed.**

Do you live in a busy neighborhood?
What is near your house? A supermarket? Your school?
What is your favorite place in your neighborhood? Why?
Do you like your neighborhood? Why?

My Neighborhood

_____

_____

_____

_____

_____

_____

_____

_____

_____

_____

Read your description to the class.

Lesson 3

In this lesson, you will learn to
- get details from a real estate ad.
- interpret abbreviations from the classified ads section.

There's a large 1 BR Apt. Furn.

🔊 **Listen and read.**

A.
Small apt. building
Large 1 BR apt. on Elm St.
Big closets. Near park. Furn.
Call 555-7363

B.
Small apt in a new bldg. W/D & A/C
2 bedrooms. Good for roommates
Near campus, trans.
7334 Summer St. Call 555-3564

C.
4 rms, LR, DR, kitchen, and BR.
Lots of light. New carpet. $850
Sunny apartment. 555-8948

Studio Apt. High ceilings

Stu
No
cl
C

2B
$
N.

La
Ne
Pa

4

Pair Match the words with their abbreviations. Write the letter in the blank.

_d_	1. apartment	a.	LR
___	2. bedroom	b.	trans.
___	3. transportation	c.	DR
___	4. dining room	d.	apt.
___	5. air conditioning	e.	W/D
___	6. building	f.	A/C
___	7. washer/dryer	g.	furn.
___	8. street	h.	bldg.
___	9. furnished	i.	BR
___	10. living room	j.	St.

1 Online

Log onto **http://www.prenhall.com/brown_activities**
The Web: Let's look around.
Grammar: What's your grammar IQ?
E-mail: My home

2 Wrap Up

<u>**Group**</u>   Work in groups of three. You have an apartment for rent. First, answer the questions below. Then, write an ad for the apartment in your notebook. Use abbreviations where possible. Compare your ad with another group's ad.

Apartment for Rent

1. Is the apartment large or small?   _____

2. How many rooms are there in the apartment?   _____

3. How many bedrooms are there?   _____

4. How many closets does the apartment have?   _____

5. Is the apartment furnished or not?   _____

6. Does the apartment have air conditioning?   _____

7. Is the apartment near a bus stop (or train)?   _____

8. How much is the rent?   _____

9. What's the phone number to call?   _____

10. What's the address of the apartment?   _____

Strategies for Success

➤ **Taking notes in English**
➤ **Making up sentences in a new context**

Get an English language newspaper in a library (or, if you are in an English-speaking country, at a newsstand). Look at the Classified Ads section. Look for items under "Apartments (or Houses or Rooms) for Rent."

1. Read five advertisements. Then, in your journal, write a short description of two places that are advertised. Don't use abbreviations.

2. Write a "pretend" advertisement for the place that you live in now.

3. When you go home tonight, walk around your house. Say the English words for as many items as possible. Walk around and practice the words, or say sentences like "This is a chair." "I like my TV." *or* "Our refrigerator is _____ (empty, full, clean, white)."

CHECKPOINT

I can	Yes!	Sometimes	Not Yet
describe an apartment.	☐	☐	☐
ask for and give locations.	☐	☐	☐
ask for a description of and describe a neighborhood.	☐	☐	☐
interpret abbreviations from the classified ads.	☐	☐	☐

Learning Preferences

Think about the work you did in this unit. Put a check next to the items that helped you learn the lessons. Put two checks next to the ones that helped a lot.

☐ ☐ Listening to the teacher
☐ ☐ Working by myself
☐ ☐ Working with a partner
☐ ☐ Working with a group
☐ ☐ Asking the teacher questions

☐ ☐ Listening to the tapes and doing exercises
☐ ☐ Reading
☐ ☐ Writing paragraphs
☐ ☐ Using the Internet

VOCABULARY

Rooms of an Apartment or House	Neighborhood	Household Items	Other Vocabulary
bathroom	apartment	bathtub	air conditioning
bedroom	avenue	bookcase	closet
dining room	building	bed	flowers
kitchen	bank	cabinet	furnished
living room	bus stop	coffee table	garbage can
	drugstore	curtains	real-estate ad
	hospital	dishwasher	rent
Prepositions of Location	library	lamp	roommate
	movie theater	microwave	shoes
across from	park	refrigerator	transportation
at	police station	rug	wastebasket
between	post office	shower	
in/on the corner of	street	sink	
in the middle of	supermarket	sofa	
in front of	trees	stove	
near		television (TV)	
next to		toilet	
on		VCR	
under		washer and dryer	

GRAMMAR SUMMARY

Prepositions of Place

	in	
	on	
	under	
The picture is	over	the desk.
	next to	
	behind	
	in front of	

The chairs are	between	the bookcases.
	around	the table.

Prepositions of Location

It's **on the corner of** Elm St. and Summer Ave.
It's **across from** the park.
My parents are **at** home.
He lives **on** Elm St.
I live **at** 245 Park Lane.
There is a supermarket **close to** the apartment.
The drugstore is **between** the post office and the police station.
Our apartment is **next to** the bus stop.

There is/are
Affirmative Statements

There	's	a television in the room.
	are	(some) pictures on the wall.

There is/are
Negative Statements

There	isn't	a television in the room.
	aren't	(any) pictures on the wall.

Yes/No Questions

Is	there	a television in the room?
Are		(any) flowers in the room?

Short Answers

Affirmative

Yes, **there is.**
Yes, **there are.**

Negative

No, **there isn't.**
No, **there aren't.**

► COMMUNICATION SUMMARY

Talking to an apartment owner
Are there any closets in the bedroom?
   Yes, there are. *or* No, there aren't.

What's the neighborhood like?

How many bedrooms are there?
   There are four. *or* Four.

Describing the location of a place
The apartment building is across from the park.

Lesson 1

In this lesson, you will learn to
- say different ways of saying the time.
- describe a present action.

I'm running late.

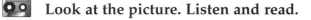
Look at the picture. Listen and read.

Lynn: Hello?

Tony: Lynn, this is Tony.

Lynn: Hi, Tony. Where are you? We're waiting for you.

Tony: What time is it?

Lynn: It's already 6 o'clock.

Tony: Oh, no! I'm really running late.

Lynn: Well, everyone is here. We're having a good time.

Tony: Without me! What's everybody doing?

Lynn: Gina and Ivan are dancing. Oscar's watching a soccer match. And Nelson's talking to Mrs. Brennan.

Tony: What's Yumiko doing?

Lynn: She's making sandwiches in the kitchen.

Tony: I have to go. By the way, I'm bringing more soda and chips.

Lynn: Good. I'll wait for you at the front gate. What time will you come?

Tony: At 6:30.

Lynn: OK. See you then.

Pair   When do you usually run late? In the morning? After school? Tell your partners about those occasions.

1 The Time

 Listen and read the following. Then draw the clock hands to show the correct time.

1:05=one-oh-five
or five after one

2:15=two-fifteen
or a quarter after two

3:35=three thirty-five
or twenty-five to four

4:45=four forty-five
or a quarter to five

5:30=five-thirty
or half past five

6:55=six fifty-five
or five to seven

2 Ask and tell the time.

Pair   Work with a partner. Ask the time. Your partner will answer. Take turns.

Examples:

A: What time is it?
B: It's 9:00 (nine o'clock).

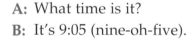

A: What time is it?
B: It's 9:05 (nine-oh-five).

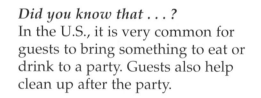

1.   2.   3.

Did you know that . . . ?
In the U.S., it is very common for guests to bring something to eat or drink to a party. Guests also help clean up after the party.

3 Hear it. Say it.

Listen and repeat the following word pairs.

thirTEEN (13)   **THIR**ty (30)   fifTEEN (15)   **FIF**ty (50)   sevenTEEN (17)   **SEV**enty (70)
fourTEEN (14)   **FOR**ty (40)   sixTEEN (16)   **SIX**ty (60)   eighTEEN (18)   **EIGH**ty (80)
                                                                  nineTEEN (19)   **NINE**ty (90)

4 What's the Bonilla family doing?

 In the chart below, write sentences about the picture. Then listen and check your answers.

What they're doing . . .	What they're not doing . . .

5 Are Mr. Bonilla and his daughter playing tennis?

Pair Work with a partner. Look at the picture above. Ask and answer *yes/no* questions.

Examples:

A: **Is** Tommy **playing** with the Frisbee?
B: No, **he isn't**.

A: **Are** Tommy and his family **eating** right now?
B: No, **they aren't**.

1. Are Mr. Bonilla and his daughter playing tennis?
2. Are they playing Frisbee?
3. Is the grandmother cooking?
4. Is the grandfather cooking?

5. Are Tommy and his mother setting the table?
6. Is the dog barking?
7. Are you asking your partner questions?

Lesson 2

In this lesson, you will learn to

- ask and describe what people are wearing.
- ask and tell what people are doing.
- follow instructions.
- talk about preferences.

He's wearing a green shirt.

Look at the picture. Listen and read.

Gina: Which one is Lynn's cousin Ken?

Yumiko: He's over there with Susana. Look! Both are wearing green and white.

Gina: Who is the woman in the corner?

Yumiko: Which one?

Gina: The one with the white blouse and red skirt. She's talking to Nelson.

Yumiko: Oh, that's Lynn's aunt, Jialing. And there's Susana's boyfriend, Roberto, over by the CD player.

Gina: The guy in the black jacket must be Silvio. By the way, where's Lynn?

Yumiko: She's waiting outside for Tony. He's coming in a few minutes.

Listen to the rest of the conversation. Label Susana, Jialing, Ken, and Roberto.

1 Word Bag: Clothes and Colors

🔊 Listen and repeat.

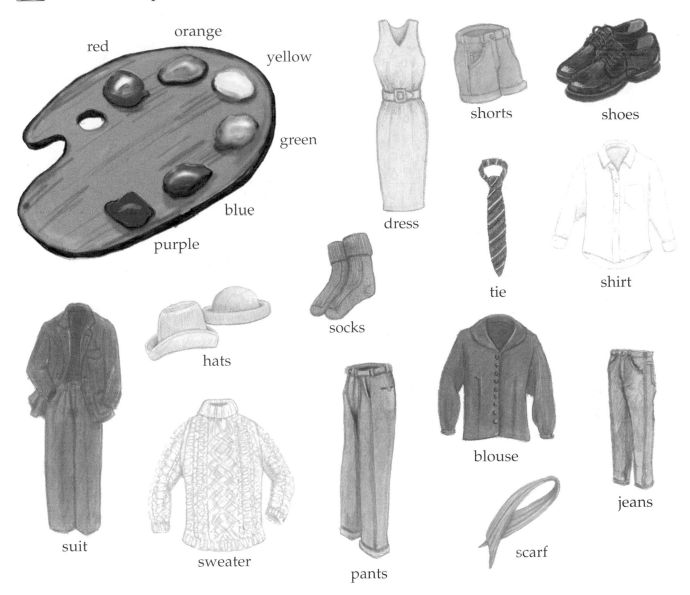

red
orange
yellow
green
blue
purple

shorts
shoes

dress
tie
shirt

socks

hats

suit
sweater
pants

blouse
scarf
jeans

2 Excuse me. I'm looking for a green dress.

🔊 Listen to the conversations.

A: Excuse me. I'm looking for a *green dress*.
B: Here's a nice *dress*.
A: But this is a *blue dress*.
B: *Blue dresses* are popular this year.
A: Yes, but I need a *green dress*.

A: Excuse me. I'm looking for some *red shorts*.
B: *Red shorts* are out of stock. Check out these *green shorts*.
A: No, I want *red shorts*.
B: *Green shorts* are in style this spring.
A: No, thanks. I don't like *green shorts*. I'll try another store.

Pair Practice the conversation. Discuss different clothing items that you want to buy.

3 Find the person.

Pair   Look at the picture on page 52. Read the sentences below. Write the name of the character. Then write what he/she is doing. The first one has been done for you.

She's wearing a purple shirt and a white skirt.

Yumiko. She's talking to Gina.

She's wearing a white blouse and red skirt.

_____

He's wearing white pants and a yellow polo shirt.

_____

She's wearing a black skirt and a red blouse.

_____

He's wearing jeans, a blue T-shirt, and a black jacket.

_____

He's wearing a blue hat, a green T-shirt, and white shorts.

_____

🔊   **Listen. Then read the words in the chart below with your teacher.**

Most nouns: add -s	Nouns ending in -x, -s, -ch, or -sh: add -es	Nouns ending in -y preceded by a consonant: change y to i and add -es	Nouns ending in -f and -fe: change f to v and add -s or -es	Irregular plurals	
hat hats	dress dresses	library libraries	scarf scarves	child	children
sock socks	watch watches	city cities	knife knives	man	men
tie ties	brush brushes	party parties	wife wives	woman	women
	box boxes				

4 What's your favorite color?

What's your favorite color? Read what psychologists say about colors.

Psychologists say that a person's favorite color can tell us something about that person's personality. People who like . . .

red are very active.

yellow are quiet.

blue are calm.

brown are very interested in the home and
    family.

green like to make good impressions on others.

purple like to be different from others.

gray are shy.

black are serious.

Group Ask six classmates about their favorite colors. Write their names under their favorite colors in the chart below.

RED	YELLOW	BLUE	BROWN	GREEN	PURPLE	GRAY	BLACK

Look for two other classmates who like the same color as you do. Answer the question: Do you agree or disagree with what these psychologists say about colors? Explain your answer.

Write your answer on the lines below. Share your answer with the class.

_____

_____

_____

_____

_____

In this lesson, you will learn to
- ask about the weather.
- describe the weather.
- describe the different seasons.
- write a letter.

The Four Seasons

 Look at the pictures as you read the paragraph. Then answer the questions.

Winter December 21–March 20

Spring March 21–June 20

In the north there are four seasons. They are winter, spring, summer, and fall. The weather in winter is cold and snowy.

In spring it is windy and rainy. In summer it is hot and sunny. It is cloudy and cool in fall, but there usually isn't any snow.

Summer June 21–September 20

Fall September 21–December 20

1. How many seasons are there in the U.S.?

2. What are the seasons?

3. What's the weather like in the winter?

4. How's the weather in the spring?

5. What's the weather like in the summer?

6. How's the weather in the fall?

Class What's the weather like where you're from? How many seasons are there? Tell the class about the weather where you're from.

1 We need clothes for every season.

Listen and repeat.

tank top

sweat shirt

bathing suit

raincoat

windbreaker

parka   tights

overcoat

jeans

jacket

gloves

jogging suit

shorts

ear muffs

down jacket

sweater

Pair Write the names of clothes under the season when they are worn. You can place some clothes in more than one season.

Spring windy/rainy	Summer sunny/hot	Fall cloudy/cool	Winter snowy/cold

2 Online

Log onto **http://www.prenhall.com/brown_activities**
The Web: It's time to check the weather.
Grammar: What's your grammar IQ?
E-mail: Summertime fun

3 Information Gap, pages 127 and 128.

<u>Pair</u>   Turn to pages 127 and 128. Follow your teacher's instructions.

4 Wrap Up

Read Gina's letter. Then write a letter to a friend. Use Gina's letter as a model.

December 12

Dear Mario,

Hi! It's winter here, my first winter in the United States! I'm waiting for the first snowfall. I can't wait to touch snow! But I also can't wait for spring because of the flowers!

So how are you? What are you doing these days? Tell me what everybody is doing. I miss everybody. Please write soon.

Your friend,
Gina

1.   Write the date. (*December 12*)

2.   Write to a friend. (*Dear Mario,*)

3.   In the first paragraph, write about yourself. Tell your friend how you are doing and what you are doing.

4.   In the second paragraph, write about the weather where you are. Tell him/her that you miss him/her.

5.   Write a closing. (*Your friend,* or *Love,*)

6.   Sign your name. (*Gina*)

Strategies for Success

➤ **Describing (in writing)**
➤ **Reading out loud**
➤ **Listening to yourself**

In this unit, you wrote to a friend. You described the weather where you are.

1. Find a place where there are people doing things (*walking, eating, drinking, laughing,* or *playing*). Sit down with a piece of paper. This time, write a short letter to someone else. Describe the weather. Also, describe what people are doing around you. Use the verbs in this unit to help you.

2. Read your letter to yourself out loud. Do this twice. The first time, try to pronounce everything correctly. The second time, look for any grammar mistakes you might have made. If you did, correct them yourself. Now, send your letter!

3. Reviewing strategies: Look back at all the strategies you have practiced so far in this course (Units 1–5). Pick one strategy to practice again.

CHECKPOINT

I can	Yes!	Sometimes	Not Yet
say the time in different ways.	☐	☐	☐
describe an ongoing action.	☐	☐	☐
ask about and describe what people are wearing.	☐	☐	☐
offer help.	☐	☐	☐
accept or decline an offer of help.	☐	☐	☐
ask about and describe the weather and seasons.	☐	☐	☐
write a letter.	☐	☐	☐

Learning Preferences

Think about the work you did in this unit. Put a check next to the items that helped you learn the lessons. Put two checks next to the ones that helped a lot.

☐ ☐ Listening to the teacher   ☐ ☐ Listening to the tapes and doing exercises
☐ ☐ Working by myself   ☐ ☐ Reading
☐ ☐ Working with a partner   ☐ ☐ Writing paragraphs
☐ ☐ Working with a group   ☐ ☐ Using the Internet
☐ ☐ Asking the teacher questions

VOCABULARY

Colors		Clothes	Weather	Action Words	
black	red	blouse	cloudy	ask	play
blue	white	dress	cold	bark	set the table
brown	yellow	hat	cool	bring	talk
gray		jacket	hot	come	visit
green		jeans	rainy	cook	wait
orange		pants	snow	dance	watch
pink		polo shirt	snowfall	eat	wear
purple		shirt	snowy	look	
		shoes	warm	make	
Seasons		shorts	windy	need	
spring		skirt			
summer		sweater			
fall					
winter					

GRAMMAR SUMMARY

Present Continuous Tense

Affirmative Sentences

I	'm (am)		
He She	's (is)	watching	TV.
You We They	're (are)		

Yes/No Questions

Are	you	
Is	he she	watching TV?
Are	they	

Negative Sentences

I	'm not		
He She	isn't	watching	TV.
We You They	aren't		

Short Answers

	I	am.
Yes,	he she	is.
	they	are.

Negative Short Answers

	I	'm not.
No,	he she	isn't.
	they	aren't.

COMMUNICATION SUMMARY

Asking and saying the time
What time is it? It's 9:00.

Asking about and describing the weather
How's the weather? *or* What's the weather like?
   It's raining.
What's the weather like in your city/country?
   It's hot in the summer and very cold in the
   winter.

Describing the different seasons
It's hot in summer and windy and cold in winter.

Asking for and describing what people are wearing
What's she wearing?
   She's wearing a blue dress.
What's he wearing?
   He's wearing black pants and a white shirt.

Offering help
May I help you? *or* Can I help you?

Accepting or declining an offer of help
Yes, I'm looking for a red sweater. *or*
No, thanks. I'm just looking.

UNIT 6

Lesson 1

In this lesson, you will learn to
- talk about daily routines at work and at home.
- ask for and give information about the days of the week.

Life in the United States isn't easy!

🔊 **Look at the pictures. Listen and read.**

1. Lynn and Yumiko are busy. They work during the day from Monday to Friday.

2. Lynn works with computers. Yumiko works in a Japanese bank. They leave work at 5:00 P.M.

3. They go to night school every Monday, Wednesday, and Friday. They meet in their English class at 6:00 P.M.

4. When they get home, they make dinner together, eat, and then wash the dishes.

5. After dinner, they do their English homework.

6. On weekends, Lynn and Yumiko clean the house and do the laundry. Life in the United States isn't easy! People are always busy!

1 What do they do?

Pair Work with a partner. Ask and answer questions about Lynn and Yumiko's schedule. Write their activities on the calendar.

A: What *do* Lynn and Yumiko *do* during the day from Monday to Friday?

B: They *work*.

A: Where *does* Yumiko *work*?

B: She *works* in a bank.

A: What *do* they *do* on weekends?

B: They *clean* the house and *do* the laundry.

SUNDAY	MONDAY	TUESDAY	WEDNESDAY	THURSDAY	FRIDAY	SATURDAY
1	2	3	4	5	6	7

OCTOBER

Pair Work with a partner. Read the abbreviations of the days of the week on the calendar below. Ask about each other's schedule. Write your activities. Use words from the list.

work	study	wake	go	do	clean

FEBRUARY

SUN.	MON.	TUES.	WED.	THURS.	FRI.	SAT.
1	2	3	4	5	6	7

I **work**.	I **don't work**.	He **works**.	He **doesn't work**.
You **work**.	You **don't work**.	She **works**.	She **doesn't work**.
We **work**.	We **don't work**.	It **works**.	It **doesn't work**.
They **work**.	They **don't work**.		

2 Do Tony and Nelson have busy schedules?

Listen for the missing words. Write them in the blanks.

On weekdays Tony and Nelson _____ busy schedules. They always _____ up
.   1   2
early and _____ jogging in the park. Then they each _____ a shower and get
.   3   4
dressed. They _____ their breakfast and _____ to work. On the weekend, they sleep
.   5   6
until noon.

Sometimes Tony _____ soccer after work. Nelson _____ home to have dinner.
.   7   8
Then they _____ to class on Monday, Wednesday, and Friday evenings. On Tuesday and
.   9
Thursday nights, Tony _____ the laundry, and Nelson _____ the house.
.   10   11

Listen to the examples.

A: **Do** Tony and Nelson **have** busy schedules?   A: **Does** Tony **get up** late?
B: Yes, **they do**.   B: No, **he doesn't**.

<u>Pair</u>   Ask and answer the questions below.

1.   Do Tony and Nelson go jogging every weekday?

2.   Do they get up early on the weekend?

3.   Do they have class on Tuesday and Thursday?

4.   Does Tony play soccer after work?

5.   When does Nelson do the laundry?

3 Information Gap Activity, pages 129 and 130.

<u>Pair</u>   Turn to pages 129 and 130. Follow your teacher's instructions.

4 Do you go to bed late on weekday nights?

<u>Group</u>   **With two other students, on your own paper write a paragraph telling what you do
and don't do during the week. Have one student write the paragraph while you all decide
what to write. Before you begin, read the example below.**

My classmates and I go to bed early during the week. We don't stay up late because we get up
very early every weekday morning. We always come to class on time. We don't arrive late because
we know our teacher wants us to be on time. We love our English class—our teacher and our
classmates! Our teacher is terrific! We don't mind working hard because we are learning so much!

5 Answer the fitness survey.

Pair How healthy are you? Answer the questions in the chart below. First answer the questions for yourself. Check *Yes, I do* or *No, I don't*. Then ask your partner the questions.

Do you . . .	You		Your Partner	
	Yes, I do.	No, I don't.	Yes, I do.	No, I don't.
1. get eight hours of sleep every night?				
2. get the same amount of sleep every night?				
3. eat fruits and vegetables every day?				
4. eat a lot of red meat?				
5. drink a lot of water every day?				
6. exercise or play sports three times a week or more?				

Use the answers above to write a paragraph on the lines below. Describe your partner's health habits.

Example:

I think my partner is a healthy person. He/she gets eight hours of sleep every night.

_____

_____

_____

_____

_____

_____

_____

_____

In this lesson, you will learn to
- ask about and compare daily routines.
- talk about frequency.

Dear Siao Yan,

 **Listen as you read Lynn's letter to Siao Yan.**

October 19

Dear Siao Yan,

How are you? I hope you're fine. I'm OK here, but I miss home. Sometimes I get very lonely.

Life in the U.S. is very different from life back home. I live with a classmate from Japan. We met at the airport. Her name is Yumiko.

We're both very busy. Yumiko works at a Japanese bank. I work at a computer company.

After work, we attend our English class. After class, we go home and make dinner. Then we study for the next English class.

We get up very early. Every day at exactly the same time we run to the bus stop. We'll miss the bus if we're one minute late! On weekends, we do the laundry and clean the house. Sometimes, we feel tired and wish we were back home. Life is more relaxed there.

How's everybody? Tell them I send my love. Write soon!

Your friend,

Lynn

Pair   Discuss these questions with a partner. Does Lynn enjoy living in the United States? Why or why not? Do you think it's easy living in another country? What stories have you heard about living in the United States? Share your ideas with the class.

1 Lynn has a busy schedule!

Pair Read Lynn's letter to Siao Yan again. Then look at each pair of pictures and choose one that shows an activity described in the letter.

1. a. Lynn and Yumiko get up early.

   b. Lynn and Yumiko get up late.

2. a. After work, Lynn goes home.

   b. After work, Lynn and Yumiko go to school.

3. a. Yumiko works in a bank.

   b. Lynn works in a bank.

4. a. Lynn and Yumiko run to the bus stop.

   b. Lynn and Yumiko walk to the bus stop.

2 Siao Yan has a more relaxed life.

Pair What's Siao Yan's life like? Make sentences about Siao Yan with the phrases below the pictures. Refer to the chart on page 67.

1. get up late

2. walk to school

3. teach kindergarten

4. go home early

5. help her mother cook dinner

6. prepare for the next day's class

Singular Subject	Verb	Plural Subject	Verb
I You	get up go study watch	We You	get up go study watch
He She It	gets up goes studies watches	They	get up go study watch

3 They have different lifestyles.

Lynn and Siao Yan have different lifestyles. Look at the chart. How about you? How often do you do these activities? Fill out the column about yourself in the chart below.

never = 0	sometimes = 1	often = 2	always = 3

Examples:

Lynn **always** gets up early.
Siao Yan **never** exercises at the gym.

Activity	LYNN	SIAO YAN	YOU
watch TV	1	2	
get up early	3	0	
get up late	0	3	
go to bed late	0	2	
exercise at the gym	1	0	
do errands	2	0	
study	2	2	

Did you know that . . . ?
Many American teenagers get jobs when they turn 16. These teenagers work after school or on weekends at supermarkets and fast-food restaurants.

Pair   On a piece of notebook paper, write sentences about Lynn and Siao Yan's different lifestyles. Use *never, sometimes, often, always*. Read your sentences to the class.

In this lesson, you will learn to
- talk about birthdays and holidays.
- read about holidays.

What special holidays do you have?

Listen and read.

New Year—China
January or February

Festival of Lights—Thailand
November

Every country has its own special holidays and festivals. In most countries, the New Year is observed on January 1 (first). In some Asian countries, like China, the New Year is observed in January or February with fireworks and parties. There are parades with huge dragons and beautiful, colorful costumes.

The Thais celebrate the Festival of Lights in November. Everywhere, little boats containing incense, a coin, and a lighted candle float down the rivers.

Independence Day—United States
July

In the United States, Independence Day, July 4 (fourth), is a time for barbecues, picnics, fireworks, and parades.

In your country, what special holiday do you have? What do you do on this day?

Write the names of three holidays that you celebrate in your own country. Next to each name, write a few words about the celebration.

Share your list with your classmates. Explain which holiday is your favorite and why.

1 Word Bag: Ordinal Numbers

 Listen and repeat.

1st first	2nd second	3rd third	4th fourth	5th fifth	6th sixth
7th seventh	8th eighth	9th ninth	10th tenth	11th eleventh	12th twelfth
13th thirteenth	14th fourteenth	15th fifteenth	16th sixteenth	17th seventeenth	18th eighteenth
19th nineteenth	20th twentieth	21st twenty-first	22nd twenty-second	23rd twenty-third	30th thirtieth

2 Guess your partner's birthday.

 Guess your partner's birthday. Listen to the instructions as you read.

1. Tell your partner to think of the number of the **day** of the month of his/her birthday.	2. Tell him/her to double that number.	3. Multiply the number by **5**.	4. Then tell him/her to add **20**.
5. Next tell him/her to multiply that number by **10**.	6. Then he/she must add the number of the month (**July** is the **seventh** month) and tell you the number.	7. Subtract **200**.	8. Now you have the **day** and the **month** of your partner's birthday!

Tell your partner his/her birthday. He/she will tell you if you're right or wrong.

3 Hear it. Say it.

 Listen as the pairs of words are read. Check (✓)the word you hear.

Sounds /t/ and /θ/

1. ( ) tenth   ( ) tent   4. ( ) fort   ( ) fourth

2. ( ) thank   ( ) tank   5. ( ) tie   ( ) thigh

3. ( ) tin   ( ) thin   6. ( ) eighth   ( ) ate

Pair   Work with a partner. Take turns saying the words with the *th-* sound first. Then, take turns saying the pairs of words to each other.

4 Online

Log onto **http://www.prenhall.com/brown_activities**
The Web: It's time to celebrate.
Grammar: What's your grammar IQ?
E-mail: Happy Birthday!

5 Wrap Up

Class Walk around the room and ask your classmates, "When's your birthday?" Then write the names and dates in the chart below.

January	July
February	August
March	September
April	October
May	November
June Susan Palmer, June 10	December

Pair Who has a birthday in the same month that you do? Talk to this classmate. Ask: What do you usually do on your birthday?

Did you know that . . . ?
In the U.S., it is not polite to ask personal questions about age, salary, or marital status.

Strategies for Success

➤ **Writing to practice sentences you've learned**
➤ **Creating opportunities to use English**

In this unit you talked about your daily routines and schedules.

1. In your journal, write about your weekday routine. Start with "I get up at _____." and continue to "Finally, I usually go to bed around _____."

2. Do you keep a personal calendar with reminders of schedules, appointments, special events, and things to do? If so, write all your entries in English so that you practice your English. If not, get a calendar and start making entries in it in English. Continue this for the rest of the semester.

3. Recycling strategies: Pick a strategy from a previous unit. Practice it again.

CHECKPOINT

I can	Yes!	Sometimes	Not Yet
talk about my daily routine.	❑	❑	❑
ask about other people's routines.	❑	❑	❑
talk about frequency.	❑	❑	❑
talk about birthdays, holidays, and other important dates on the calendar.	❑	❑	❑
write a description of my daily life.	❑	❑	❑
talk about differences.	❑	❑	❑
talk about health habits.	❑	❑	❑

Learning Preferences

Think about the work you did in this unit. Put a check next to the items that helped you learn the lessons. Put two checks next to the ones that helped a lot.

❑ ❑ Listening to the teacher
❑ ❑ Working by myself
❑ ❑ Working with a partner
❑ ❑ Working with a group
❑ ❑ Asking the teacher questions

❑ ❑ Listening to the tapes and doing exercises
❑ ❑ Reading
❑ ❑ Writing paragraphs
❑ ❑ Researching the Internet

VOCABULARY

Months	Days		Adverbs
January	Sunday	Sun.	always
February	Monday	Mon.	early
March	Tuesday	Tues.	every
April	Wednesday	Wed.	every day
May	Thursday	Thurs.	late
June	Friday	Fri.	never
July	Saturday	Sat.	often
August			on Monday
September			sometimes
October			
November			
December			

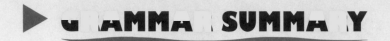
SIMPLE PRESENT TENSE

Subject Pronoun	Verb	Adverb of Frequency
I You	**work**	
He She It	**works**	often.

Subject Pronoun	Verb	Adverb of Frequency
We You		
They	**work**	often.

Helping Verb	Subject Pronoun	Verb	Adverb of Frequency
Do	you we they	**work**	often?
Does	he she it		

Affirmative Response		
Yes,	I we they	**do.**
	he she it	**does.**

Negative Response		
No,	I we they	**don't.**
	he she it	**doesn't.**

► COMMUNICATION SUMMARY

Requesting and giving information about important dates
What day is today?
   (It's) Monday.
When is your birthday?
   (It's) September 24.

Talking about activities during the week
They work from Monday to Friday.
On weekends, Lynn and Yumiko clean the house.

Asking about people's schedules
Do they have class on Tuesday and Thursday?
   No, they don't.
Do they work every day?
   Yes, they do.

Explaining differences
Tony and Nelson have jobs, but Oscar doesn't have a job.

UNIT 7

Lesson 1

In this lesson, you will learn to
- talk about availability of things.
- talk about quantities of food items.
- ask for locations in a supermarket.

I'm making a grocery list.

🔊 **Listen and read.**

Yumiko: What are you doing?

Lynn: I'm making a grocery list. Some friends are coming for dinner, and I'm making a chicken and rice dish. I need some things from the supermarket.

Yumiko: Chicken and rice? What else is in it?

Lynn: Carrots, tomatoes, mushrooms, green peppers, onions, and garlic.

Yumiko: I know we don't have any green peppers or garlic. And we need some mushrooms, onions, and carrots.

Lynn: What about salt and oil?

Yumiko: Let's see. We have some salt, but we don't have any black pepper or oil.

Lynn: OK. And, of course, we need to buy the chicken. Do we need anything else?

Yumiko: Yes. We need some coffee, orange juice, and bread for breakfast tomorrow. And there isn't any milk. We need a lot of things. Let's go shopping together. I can help.

Pair Do you have a favorite dish you like to prepare? Tell your partner what you need to make it.

1 Word Bag: Food Items

Pair   Read the conversation on page 73 again. Put a check ✓ after each item needed and an ✗ after those that are not needed.

		Lynn and Yumiko need some . . .	They don't need any . . .
1.	chicken	✓	___
2.	rice	___	___
3.	soup	___	✗
4.	milk	___	___
5.	black pepper	___	___
6.	green peppers	___	___
7.	onions	___	___
8.	potato	___	___
9.	carrots	___	___
10.	salt	___	___
11.	beans	___	___
12.	coffee	___	___
13.	orange juice	___	___
14.	bread	___	___
15.	milk	___	___
16.	sugar	___	___

Write the above food items in the correct section of the chart.

Count Nouns	Noncount Nouns
potatoes	rice

Add more food words to the lists above.

cookies	flour	bananas	meat
butter	mangoes	apples	cheese
tomatoes	eggs	lettuce	oil

2 What do we have?

Look at the picture as you listen to the conversation. The items Lynn has are marked with a ✓. The things she doesn't have are marked with an ✗.

Examples:

> A: black pepper
> B: black pepper ✗; salt ✓

Yumiko: Is there any *black pepper*?

Lynn: There isn't any *black pepper*, but there's some *salt*.

Yumiko: I need *pepper*. Let's get some.

> A: carrots
> B: carrots ✗; green beans ✓

Yumiko: Are there any *carrots*?

Lynn: There aren't any *carrots*, but there are some *green beans*.

Yumiko: No, I can't use *green beans*. Let's buy some *carrots*.

Pair Work with a partner. Following the examples above, ask and answer questions about the things Yumiko and Lynn have (✓) and don't have (✗) in their cupboard. Use the foods listed below.

1. A: mushrooms

   B: mushrooms ✗, onions ✓

2. A: green peppers

   B: green peppers ✗, red peppers ✓

3. A: garlic

   B: garlic ✗, onions ✓

4. A: coffee

   B: coffee ✗, soda ✓

3 Information Gap Activity, pages 131 and 132.

Turn to pages 131 and 132. Follow your teacher's instructions.

4 Do you have brown rice?

Look around the grocery store as you listen to the conversation.

Lynn: Excuse me. Do you have **green peppers**?

Clerk: Yes, we do.

Lynn: Where are **they**?

Clerk: Aisle 1.

Yumiko: Do you have brown **rice**?

Clerk: No, we don't, but we have white **rice**.

Yumiko: Where is **it**?

Clerk: Aisle 2.

Pair Work with a partner. Ask and answer questions about where food items are located. Follow the examples above.

1. salad dressing ✗

    mayonnaise ✓

2. fresh fish ✗

    frozen fish ✓

3. lettuce ✗

    cabbage ✓

5 Where's the meat?

Listen to the conversation in the supermarket. Write the food words in the aisles where they belong.

1. oil
2. salt
3. green peppers
4. onions
5. bread
6. coffee
7. milk
8. oranges
9. chicken

Aisle 1	Aisle 2	Aisle 3

Pair Ask where some of the food items are in the supermarket. Follow the model below.

A: Excuse me. Where is/are the _____?

B: It's/They're in Aisle _____.

6 A family that eats together . . .

Read the story.

My family likes different kinds of food. To start with, Dad is a meat-and-potato kind of guy. **How much** meat does he eat every week? **A lot**! His favorite dinner is steak with **a lot** of gravy and a baked potato with **some** cheese on it. But Mom makes him eat **a little** fish and **a few** vegetables now and then.

Mom is a vegetarian. She'll eat anything that comes from plants. Our refrigerator is full of oranges, bananas, apples, tofu, and green leafy vegetables.

My older brother is the junk-food king. He loves doughnuts, burgers, and french fries. But Mom doesn't buy **any** fast food because it contains **a lot** of fat. My brother doesn't care. He works at Big Burger after school. There he can have as **many** burgers and as **much** cola as he wants after work. As for me, I'm easy to please.

Write about your family's eating habits. What kinds of food does your family eat a lot of? What kinds don't they eat? Use *many, much, some, a lot of, a few/few,* **and** *any* **where appropriate.**

_____   _____

_____   _____

_____   _____

_____   _____

Pair   With a partner, plan a menu for your dinner. Write down the foods you've chosen. Share your menu with the class and explain why you've picked these foods.

Lesson 2

In this lesson, you will learn to
- ask about prices.
- read food advertisements.
- talk about food containers.

This Week Only!

🔊 Listen as you read the prices in the ad. Then read the conversation.

Lynn: How much is the chicken?

Yumiko: It's on sale. It's $1.09 (a dollar nine) a pound.

Lynn: That's a good deal. What about tomatoes?

Yumiko: They're not on sale, but tomato sauce is four cans for 99¢ (ninety-nine cents).

Lynn: No, I want fresh tomatoes. How about green peppers? Are they on sale?

Yumiko: Yes, green peppers are five for a dollar.

Lynn: Don't forget to cut out the coupons. We can save money if we use them.

Do you use coupons when you go to the supermarket? If not, try using them for a week and see how much you save. Tell the class about your experience.

1 Word Bag: Containers and Quantities

List each food below the appropriate container. A food item can be in more than one column.

can	bottle/jar	box	bag

beans   mayonnaise   soda   crackers   coffee   salt   rice   peas   tea

pepper   oil   candy   jam   vinegar   cookies   mustard   cereal   soup

Add three more food items to each column.

Match the quantities in the list with the foods below. Write the letter of the food item on the line.

1. _____ a **loaf** of
2. _____ a **head** of
3. _____ a **gallon** of
4. _____ a **jar** of
5. _____ a **box** of
6. _____ a **pound (lb.)** of
7. _____ a **dozen**
8. _____ a **bunch** of
9. _____ a **bag** of

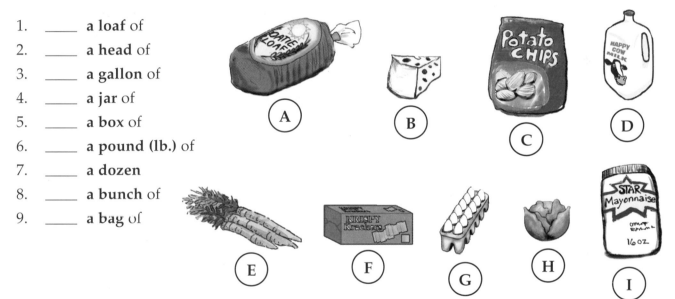

2 Hear it. Say it.

Listen. Circle the word that you hear.

Sounds /a/ and /ə/

1. a. cop   b. cup
2. a. cut   b. cot
3. a. nut   b. knot
4. a. jug   b. jog
5. a. hot   b. hut
6. a. bunch   b. box

3 What's the price?

🔊 Look at the ad on page 78. Listen to the conversation.

A: How much are *the carrots*?

B: They're *ninety-nine cents a bunch.*

A: How much is *the bread*?

B: *A dollar twenty-nine a loaf.*

Pair Work with a partner. Ask and answer questions about the prices in the ad on page 78.

4 How much are the eggs?

🔊 A man is in a small grocery store. Listen to the conversation. Write the prices.

eggs _____ a dozen

margarine _____ a pound

cabbage _____ a head

potatoes _____ a bag

bread _____ a loaf

jam _____ a jar

Did you know that . . . ?
In the United States, you can save a lot on grocery bills. How? Use coupons! Shoppers cut coupons out of newspapers and other ads. They take the coupons when they go shopping. The discounts are given at the cash register.

Add the prices and write the total below.

TOTAL _____

5 Let's have a party!

Class Plan a class party. Discuss the kinds of food you want. Ask everyone to volunteer to bring something—food, drinks, paper plates, napkins, etc. Choose a secretary to go around the group to find out what everyone plans to bring, and write the information in a chart like the one below in his/her notebook.

Name	Party Food or Item

As the secretary reports to the class, one student or your teacher will write the information on the board. If volunteers are bringing too much of the same thing, discuss some other choices and make some changes.

Lesson 3

In this lesson, you will learn to
- follow directions in a recipe.
- write a recipe.
- determine the sequence in a series of recipe instructions.

This is a favorite family recipe.

Listen and read.

Sugar Nut Cookies

1 cup of margarine or butter
1 cup of sugar
2 eggs
1 teaspoon of vanilla extract

2 ½ cups of flour
2 teaspoons of baking soda
½ teaspoon of salt
1 cup chopped nuts

First, heat the oven to 350 degrees. Mix the margarine, sugar, eggs, and vanilla extract in a bowl. Next, stir in the flour, baking soda, and salt. Then pour in the nuts. Drop teaspoonfuls of the batter on a cookie sheet. Bake the cookies for about 10 minutes or until brown. Put them on a plate and let cool.

1 First, heat the oven.

First, read the recipe card above. Number the pictures to show the order of the recipe steps. Then write the action word under each picture.

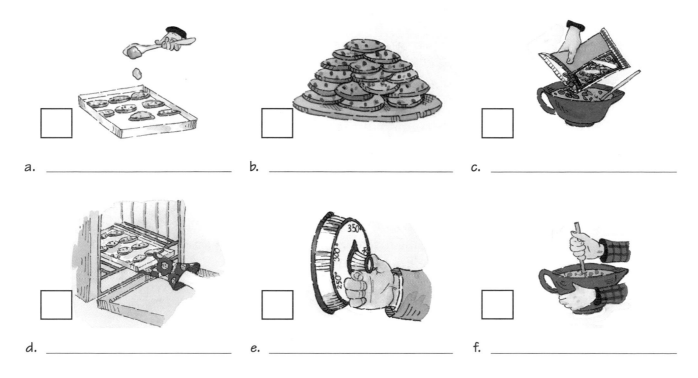

a. _____

b. _____

c. _____

d. _____

e. _____

f. _____

2 How much margarine do you need?

Pair   Read the recipe again. Ask and answer questions with *How much* and *How many*.

Example:

A: *How much* margarine do you need to make the cookies?
B: You need *one cup*.

1. sugar
2. vanilla extract
3. chopped nuts
4. eggs
5. flour
6. baking soda

3 Online

Log onto **http://www.prenhall.com/brown_activities**
The Web: Try this in your kitchen.
Grammar: What's your grammar IQ?
E-mail: My favorite food

4 Wrap Up

Group   Work in groups of three. First, decide on a simple dish — cookie recipe, cake, meat dish, pasta, noodles, rice dish, soup, etc. — that everybody in the group knows how to prepare.

Next, write down the step-by-step directions on an index card. Use the words *First, Next, Then*. You might want to prepare the dish with your group and bring the food to class.

Finally, exchange recipes with other groups.

Did you know that . . . ?
In the United States, potluck parties are popular, especially in the summer months. Friends and families come to the party with food and drinks so that the host doesn't have to do all the cooking.

Strategies for Success

➤ **Connecting new words with real-life images**
➤ **Finding out the word for something**
➤ **Writing to practice English from your lessons**

In this unit you learned the names of food items and about prices and shopping.

1. Go through your kitchen cabinets and refrigerator to see if you know the English word for everything you see. Say the words aloud as you see the items.

2. Make a list in your journal of all the food items you identified. Make another list (in your native language) of items that you did not know the English word for. With your partner, find out the English word.

3. In your journal, write one paragraph about your favorite foods and why you like them, and another paragraph about foods you don't like and why. Share with a partner.

CHECKPOINT

I can	Yes!	Sometimes	Not Yet
talk about availability.	☐	☐	☐
talk about quantities.	☐	☐	☐
ask for and give locations in a supermarket.	☐	☐	☐
ask about and give prices.	☐	☐	☐
talk about favorite foods.	☐	☐	☐
follow and write a recipe.	☐	☐	☐

Think about the work you did in this unit. Put a check (✓) next to the items that helped you learn the lessons. Put two checks next to the ones that helped a lot.

☐ ☐ Listening to the teacher   ☐ ☐ Listening to the tapes and doing exercises
☐ ☐ Working by myself   ☐ ☐ Reading
☐ ☐ Working with a partner   ☐ ☐ Writing paragraphs
☐ ☐ Working with a group   ☐ ☐ Researching the Internet
☐ ☐ Asking the teacher questions

VOCABULARY

Food-Related Words

aisle	chicken	jar	potatoes
bag	container	lettuce	poultry
baking soda	cookies	loaf	pound
bananas	cookie sheet	margarine	price
bar	coupon	mayonnaise	quart
black pepper	cup	meat	recipe
bottle	doughnuts	mixture	salad dressing
bowl	dozen	mushrooms	sale
box	eggs	nuts	salt
bunch	flour	oil	shopping list
burgers	fruit	onions	soda
butter	gallon	orange juice	soup
cabbage	1/2 (a half)	oranges	sugar
can	garlic	oven	supermarket
candy	green beans	package	teaspoon
carrots	green peppers	peas	tomatoes
celery	head	pint	vanilla extract
cheese	jam	plate	vegetables

Action Words

add
bake
cool
count
drop
heat
mix
put
stir (in)
want (to)

▶ GRAMMAR SUMMARY

Count Nouns

tomato	tomatoes
potato	potatoes
red pepper	red peppers
onion	onions

Some and Any
We have **some** salt.
There isn't **any** coffee.
There aren't **any** eggs.

A lot of, Much, and Many
We need **a lot of** things.
There are **many** bananas.

She doesn't buy **much** meat.
How much does he eat?
And **how many** burgers does he eat?

A little, A few
But Mom gets him to eat **a little** fish and **a few**
vegetables now and then.

Noncount Nouns

rice	a bag of rice
flour	a bag of flour
black pepper	a can of pepper
milk	a gallon of milk

Questions and Negative Responses
Is there **any** black pepper?
    No, there isn't **any** pepper.
Are there **any** carrots?
    No, there aren't **any** carrots.

Who eats **a lot of** vegetables?
Who doesn't eat **any** vegetables?

Quantities
a bag of rice; 20 pounds/kilos of rice
a bunch of carrots
a dozen eggs
a quart/gallon of milk
a bottle of vinegar
a box of cookies

▶ COMMUNICATION SUMMARY

Talking about availability
Is there any black pepper?
    There isn't any black pepper, but
    there's some salt.
Do we have much cooking oil?
    No, we don't have much.
    No, there isn't any.
    Yes, we have a lot.
Do you have any oranges at home?
    No, I don't.

Asking for locations in a grocery store
Excuse me. Where can I find cooking oil?
    In Aisle 2.

Asking about prices
How much is a bag of candy?
    99¢ a bag.
How much are eggs this week?
    They're $1.19 a dozen.

Talking about favorite foods
My brother loves burgers.

Lesson 1

In this lesson, you will learn to

- ask for and give information on transportation and travel.
- recognize travel signs.

What time does the next bus leave?

Gina is going to visit her brother. Listen and read.

Ticket agent: Can I help you?

Gina: Yes. Which bus goes to Baytown, please?

Ticket agent: Bus number 45.

Gina: And where can I buy a ticket?

Ticket agent: Right here. I sell tickets.

Gina: What time does the next bus leave?

Ticket agent: It leaves at 8:00 and arrives at 11:15A.M. Do you want a round-trip or a one-way ticket?

Gina: Round-trip, please.

Ticket agent: That will be $50.

Gina: Here you are. Which gate is it?

Ticket agent: Gate 17.

Gina: Thanks. What time is it now?

Ticket agent: It's 7:45.

Gina: 7:45! I'd better hurry! I don't want to miss the bus.

Pair Read the conversation with a partner.

1 Hear it. Say it.

Listen. Then read each question aloud.

Questions with *or*

1. Do you want a round-trip or a one-way ticket?
2. Are you paying by cash or credit card?
3. Is it Gate 7 or Gate 17?
4. Do we take the bus or the train?
5. Do you want first class or coach?

2 Word Bag: Types of Transportation

Write the transportation words in the correct category.

ship   train   helicopter
sailboat   subway   jet
truck   airplane   car
canoe   motorcycle
bus   bicycle

Land	Water	Air

3 What does this sign mean?

Match the sign with what it means.

____ 1. baggage claim

____ 2. gas

____ 3. no parking

____ 4. no smoking

____ 5. pedestrian crossing

____ 6. do not enter

____ 7. ground transportation

____ 8. restaurant

____ 9. yield

____ 10. access for handicapped

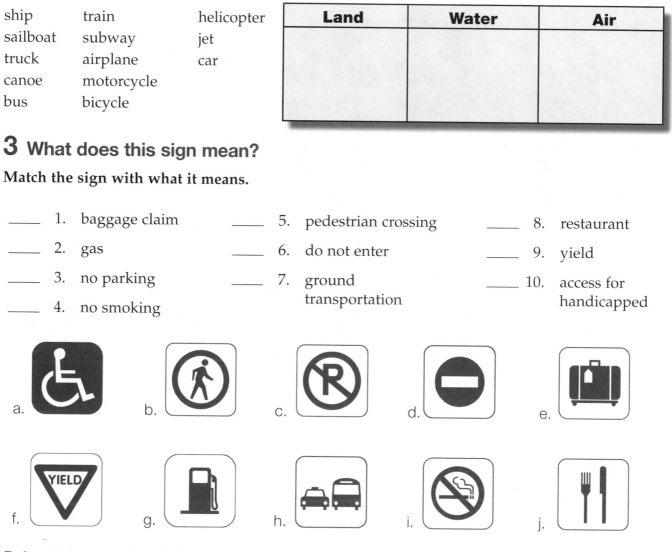

a.   b.   c.   d.   e.

f.   g.   h.   i.   j.

Pair Point to a sign. Take turns asking and telling what each sign means.

A: What does this sign mean?   B: It means *No Parking.*

4 What time does the next bus leave?

Listen and fill in the bus numbers and times that are missing from the bus schedule.

BUS NUMBER	DEPARTURES	ARRIVALS
_____	6:15 A.M.	____ P.M.
_____	____ A.M.	____ P.M.
_____	9:00 A.M.	3:00 P.M.
_____	12:00 P.M.	6:00 P.M.
_____	____ P.M.	____ P.M.

Did you know that . . . ?
In Japan, in some train stations, there are employees, *ekiin-san*, whose job is to push commuters into the train so everybody can get in during rush hours.

Pair   Look at the bus schedule above and practice the conversation below.

It's 6:00 in the morning.

A: May I help you?

B: Yes. What time does the first bus leave for Houston?

A: At _____.

B: And when does it arrive?

A: At _____.

B: Thank you.

A: You're welcome.

Group   Now plan a class trip. Call the bus or train station for information about schedules and prices. Share your plans and information with the class.

5 Information Gap Activity, pages 133 and 134.

Turn to pages 133 and 134. Follow your teacher's instructions.

6 It was my favorite trip ever!

Write a short paragraph about your favorite trip. Follow the model below.

   My favorite trip was my trip here to the United States. I traveled by plane.
It was my first plane ride. It was a long trip. It took 10 hours. I was excited.
I was coming to my new home.

_____

_____

_____

_____

Read your paragraph to the class.

In this lesson, you will learn to

- get information on movie schedules.
- talk about leisure activities.
- talk about routines.

What's playing at the movies?

While Gina is visiting her brother, her friends are going to the movies. Listen as you read the conversation.

Tony: What's playing at the movies tonight?

Oscar: Hmm, let's see. There's *The Invasion*.

Lynn: I don't really like science fiction.

Tony: I don't like science fiction much either.

Oscar: What about this love story? It stars Vanessa Fuentes.

Lynn: No. I don't like love stories.

Tony: I don't like love stories either.

Lynn: Hey! What about *I Thought; He Thought*? It's a comedy.

Tony: Yeah. I enjoy comedies. How about you, Oscar?

Oscar: Fine with me. I like comedies, too.

Tony: Yumiko? Do you like comedies?

Yumiko: Of course! Doesn't everyone? Love stories and science fiction are OK, too.

Class How about you? Tell the class about a movie you really enjoyed.

1 Tony likes comedies.

🎧 Listen to the sentences. Make your own sentences about each person in the chart.
✓ = like; x = doesn't like

LOVE STORY	COMEDY	SCIENCE FICTION	ACTION
Lynn ✗	Lynn ✓	Lynn ✗	Lynn ✗
Yumiko ✓	Yumiko ✓	Yumiko ✓	Yumiko ✗
Tony ✗	Tony ✓	Tony ✗	Tony ✓
Oscar ✗	Oscar ✓	Oscar ✓	Oscar ✓

Did you know that . . . ?
In some U.S. towns and cities, you pay only half the regular price of a movie ticket if you go between 1:00 and 5:00 in the afternoon.

Examples:

Yumiko **likes** love stories, **but** Oscar **likes** comedies.

Tony **likes** comedies, **and** Lynn **likes** comedies, **too**.

Lynn **doesn't like** love stories, **and** Oscar **doesn't like** love stories **either**.

_____

_____

_____

_____

2 Class Survey

Group Work with three classmates. Write your names at the top of the chart below. Check (✓) the chart to show what kinds of movies you and your classmates like.

Examples:

A: What kinds of movies do you like?

B: I like *comedies* and *science fiction*.

or

A: Do you like *comedies*?

B: Yes, I do. *or* No, I don't.

Category				
Love stories				
Comedies				
Science fiction				
Action				

Group Write sentences about your group. Use the information in your chart.

1. _____

2. _____

3. _____

3 Take a message, please.

Listen to each message. Write the message on the message slip.

1.
```
For:_____
Date:_____   Time:_____ A.M./P.M.
  • • • • • WHILE YOU WERE OUT • • • • •
MR./MS. _____
Phone Number: _____
Message:_____
_____
```

2.
```
For:_____
Date:_____   Time:_____ A.M./P.M.
  • • • • • WHILE YOU WERE OUT • • • • •
MR./MS. _____
Phone Number: _____
Message:_____
_____
```

3.
```
For:_____
Date:_____   Time:_____ A.M./P.M.
  • • • • • WHILE YOU WERE OUT • • • • •
MR./MR. _____
Phone Number: _____
Message:_____
_____
```

4.
```
For:_____
Date:_____   Time:_____ A.M./P.M.
  • • • • • WHILE YOU WERE OUT • • • • •
MR./MS. _____
Phone Number: _____
Message:_____
_____
```

4 What's on Channel 2 at 6:30 P.M.?

Look at the following TV monitors. Write the name of each type of TV program.

| game show | news | talk show | soap opera | comedy | sports |

_____

_____

Look at the TV guide below.

	4:00 P.M.	4:30 P.M.	5:00 P.M.	5:30 P.M.	6:00 P.M.	6:30 P.M.
2	People's Court		News		News	Superman
4	Geraldo		News		News	News
5	Simpsons	Martin	Local News		Home Improvement	Living Single
6	Public Access		Valley Journal		Public Access	
7	Oprah		News		World News	Local News
9	Amor mìo		Noticiero		Esmeralda	
11	Sesame Street		Jim Lehrer		News	

Pair Ask and answer questions about the TV schedule.

A: What's on Channel 2 at *6:30*?
B: *Superman*.
A: What time is *Oprah* on?
B: At *4:00*. Do you watch *Oprah*?
A: Every day! I love Oprah's show! How about you? Do you like talk shows?
B: Not really. In fact, I hate talk shows!

Pair Tell your partner what your favorite TV shows are and why.

Lesson 3

In this lesson, you will learn to
- write a series of actions in proper sequence.
- talk about your school or work.

It's not all fun and glamour.

🎧 Many people think a movie star's life is fun and exciting. Listen to and read the interview. Find out what a movie star's life is really like.

Entertainment Magazine Thursday, November 26

A Day in the Life of a Movie Star

An Interview with Vanessa Fuentes

Hollywood —"A movie star's life is not all fun and glamour. Every day is hectic," says actress Vanessa Fuentes. "When we're shooting a picture, I usually get up at 4:00 A.M. First, I do my exercises and take a shower. Then my hairdresser and makeup artist work on me for three hours. After that, we shoot a scene until 8 or 9 at night, sometimes until midnight. We often shoot the same scene twenty times. When it's perfect, we get a short break to have something to eat. It's a long, hard day.

"A movie star's life is not all fun and glamour. Every day is hectic."

"On a good day, I go home around 9 o'clock. I study my script and go to bed at 11. Who says a movie star's life is easy?" ★ ★ ★

Group Work in groups of three to five. Discuss the good and bad sides of being a movie star. Are the hard work and irregular hours worth it? Share your opinions with the class.

1 After that, I have breakfast.

Write about your day. Answer these questions. Use the words on the left to connect your ideas. Use the article on page 92 as an example.

Next
After that
Then
and then

1. What time do you get up?
2. What do you do next?
3. What time do you work/study? (I work/study from . . . until . . .)
4. What time do you get home?

5. What time do you have dinner?
6. What do you do after that?
7. What time do you go to bed?

_____

_____

_____

_____

2 Are you a night person or a day person?

Pair   Compare your answers from Activity 1 with a partner's answers. Then ask the questions in the chart. Check *Me* or *My Partner* for each.

	Me	My Partner
1. Who gets up first?		
2. Who goes to bed last?		
3. Who spends the most time at school/work?		
4. Who spends time at work/school in the evening?		
5. Who is a night person?		
6. Who is a day person?		

Are you a day person or a night person? Which kind of person is your partner? On a piece of paper, write three sentences to tell your class what you have found out about each other.

3 Online

Log onto **http://www.prenhall.com/brown_activities**
The Web: Are you bored? Do something interesting.
Grammar: What's your grammar IQ?
E-mail: Just for fun

4 Wrap Up

Group Work in a group of three to five. Make a survey of how your group members spend their free time. Ask: What do you do during your free time? Write your classmates' names and in the appropriate box, write the number of hours a week they spend doing each activity.

Name	Read	Watch TV	Exercise or play sports	Attend concerts or sports events	Hang out with friends	Total hours

Class Add up the group totals. Report them to the class. As a class, make a poster of the results of your survey. Discuss as a class: Do you and your classmates spend your leisure time wisely? What, in your opinion, is wise use of leisure time?

Group Choose one member of the group to report your findings to the class. Our group spends ____ hours reading, ____ hours watching TV, etc.

Strategies for Success

➤ Reading authentic material in English
➤ Creating interesting conversations with your partner

In this unit you have learned about travel, transportation, and leisure activities.

1. With your partner go to a travel agency or visit a website and ask for some information about a country you would like to visit (or go to school in, or do business in). Ask for a brochure written in English. Now, take notes on specific tours or excursions that you would like to take. Make a specific plan for a trip, complete with schedules of various forms of transportation, hotels, etc.

2. Tell the class about the trip you have planned. If you don't understand something a classmate is saying, make sure you ask questions to find out.

3. Recycling strategies: Pick another strategy that you liked from a previous unit. Practice it again.

CHECKPOINT

I can	Yes!	Sometimes	Not Yet
ask for and give information on transportation.	☐	☐	☐
talk about daily routines.	☐	☐	☐
talk about movies and TV.	☐	☐	☐
ask and tell the meaning of travel signs.	☐	☐	☐
write a series of events in proper sequence.	☐	☐	☐

Learning Preferences

Think about the work you did in this unit. Put a check (✓) next to the items that helped you learn the lessons. Put two checks next to the ones that helped a lot.

☐ ☐ Listening to the teacher
☐ ☐ Working by myself
☐ ☐ Working with a partner
☐ ☐ Working with a group
☐ ☐ Asking the teacher questions

☐ ☐ Listening to the tapes and doing exercises
☐ ☐ Reading
☐ ☐ Writing paragraphs
☐ ☐ Using the Internet

VOCABULARY

Transportation	Nouns	Verbs	Adjectives
airplane	arrival	arrive	first class
bicycle	cash	leave (for)	hectic
bus	coach	miss	irregular
canoe	comedy	sell	one-way
car	credit card	spend	round-trip
helicopter	departure		
jet	destination		
motorcycle	leisure		
sailboat	love story		
ship	movie star		
subway	script		
train	ticket		
truck			

► GRAMMAR SUMMARY

SIMPLE PRESENT

**Simple Present Tense:
Information (*Wh-*) Questions**

Question word +	*do/does* +	Subject +	Main Verb	
When	**do**	you we they	**leave**	for Houston?
	does	he she the bus		

Response

Subject +	Verb	
I We You They	**leave**	at 9:00.
He She It	**leaves**	at 9:00.

Too and *Either*
Lynn **likes** comedies, and Tony likes comedies, **too**.
Lynn **doesn't like** love stories, and Oscar doesn't like them, **either**.

Then, After that, Next, and *Then*
First, I do my exercises. **Then** my hairdresser does my hair. **After that**, we shoot a scene **and then** take a short break.

But
Oscar likes love stories, **but** Tony likes comedies.

► COMMUNICATION SUMMARY

Offering help
Can I help you?

Asking for transportation information
What time does the next bus leave for Houston?
  At 9:00.
When does it arrive?
  At 3:00 P.M. *or* At 3:00 in the afternoon.
What does this sign mean?
  It means *No Parking*.

Talking about leisure activities
What do you do during your free time?
  I read a book.

Talking about movies and TV shows
What kind of movies/TV programs do you like?
  I like comedies.
What's playing at the movies tonight?
What's on Channel 2 at 6:30?

Lesson 1

In this lesson, you will learn to
- fill out a job application.
- ask and talk about abilities.
- ask for confirmation.

Here's Gina's job application.

Listen and read.

E M P L O Y M E N T   A P P L I C A T I O N

First Name _Gina_   Last Name _Poggi_

Date of Birth _8/25/1976_   Place of Birth _Naples, Italy_

Social Security No. or ID Card No. _759-53-3452_

Home Address _7646 Hills Ave. No. 125, San Francisco, CA 94131_

Phone Number _(415) 555-3255_

Job Title _Secretary_

Your Degree _High School Diploma_

What languages can you speak? _Italian and English_

Tell us about yourself: _I am a student at the World Culture Center. I'm studying business and English. I can speak Italian and English and can understand Spanish. I am a friendly person. I work well with other people._

Check your abililties.

☑ Use a computer   ☐ Use a photocopy machine   ☐ Have good phone skills

☐ Use a fax machine   ☑ Speak English well   ☑ Speak another language   ☑ Type

☐ Work well with others   ☑ Can work on weekends   ☐ Can work nights   ☐ Drive

---

What can Gina do? Write five sentences telling what Gina can do.

1. _____

2. _____

3. _____

4. _____

5. _____

1 Can you drive?

Pair Ask and answer questions about the pictures below. Follow the models. Use the verbs in the list.

Examples: A: **Can** she **play** basketball?   A: **Can** she **type** well?

   B: Yes, she **can**.   B: No, she **can't**.

drive	type	open	play
sleep	read	swim	ride

2 He can cook!

Group Ask two classmates what they *can* or *can't* do. Put a check (✓) for each activity you or they can do.

Example: Can you *swim*?
   Yes, I can.
   No, I can't.

Abilities	You	Classmate 1	Classmate 2
play a musical instrument			
type			
use a computer			
cook			
play tennis			
sing			
dance			
rollerblade			

Share the information with the class. Use *can* or *can't*.

3 Hear it. Say it.

Listen. Then repeat.

1. Can you swim?
2. Can she drive?
3. Does he (name of classmate) take the bus?
4. Are you in the evening class?
5. Do we all understand the lesson?

Pair Ask your partner the questions. Have him/her answer.

4 Fill out this form, please.

Pair Read the job application form on page 97 again. With a partner, choose one of the following jobs to apply for: English tutor, secretary, receptionist, security guard, or cashier. Then ask your partner the questions below. Fill out the application form with his/her responses.

1. What's your first name? Your middle name? Your last name?
2. What's your date of birth?
3. What's your place of birth?
4. What's your home address?
5. What's your home phone number?
6. What's your Social Security, identification card, or driver's license number?
7. What job title are you applying for?
8. What's your degree? (high school diploma, college degree, etc.)
9. What languages can you speak?

EMPLOYMENT APPLICATION

First Name _____ Last Name _____

Date of Birth _____ Place of Birth _____

Social Security No. or ID Card No. _____

Home Address _____

Phone Number _____

Job Title _____

Your Degree _____

What languages can you speak? _____

Check your abililties.

☐ Use a computer ☐ Use a photocopy machine ☐ Have good phone skills
☐ Use a fax machine ☐ Speak English well ☐ Speak another language ☐ Type
☐ Work well with others ☐ Can work on weekends ☐ Can work nights ☐ Drive

5 Wanted: An Excellent English Teacher

🔊 The school needs a new English teacher. Three people have applied for the job. Listen and read.

A.

> My name's John Wright. I have a Master's degree in English literature. I can speak German as well as English. I love teaching English. I always have fun in class, and my students have a lot of fun also.

1. What degree does John Wright have? _____

2. What languages can he speak? _____

3. Does John Wright enjoy teaching? _____

B.

> I'm Farid Ibrahim. I'm from Egypt. I can speak English, Arabic, and French. I have a university degree in teaching English as a Foreign Language. I have many years of experience as an English grammar teacher. I can stay after hours to help students.

1. Where is Farid Ibrahim from? _____

2. How many languages does he speak? _____

3. What can he do after hours? _____

C.

> My name is Mary Franklin. I can speak Chinese as well as English. My husband is from China. I have two children. They can speak both English and Chinese. I can sing and play the guitar.

1. What languages can Mary Franklin speak? _____

2. Where is Mary's husband from? _____

3. What can she do? _____

Group Work in groups of three. Answer the questions about these job applications. Now discuss with your group: "Who is the best candidate?" Explain your answer.

Name of applicant: _____

Reasons for your choice of candidate:

1. _____

2. _____

Lesson 2

In this lesson, you will learn to
- ask for and give personal information at an interview.
- respond to interview questions.
- ask for confirmation.
- ask and talk about frequency.

I'm here for the interview.

Listen and read.

Gina: Good morning. My name is Gina Poggi. I'm here for the interview.

Mr. Brown: Hi. I'm Michael Brown. Please have a seat.

Gina: Thank you.

Mr. Brown: Let me go over your application. I see that you want to be a secretary at this bank. Can you tell me a little about yourself?

Gina: I'm a student. I'm studying English right now. I sometimes work as my uncle's secretary in his small company.

Mr. Brown: How many words can you type a minute?

Gina: Seventy words a minute. I seldom make mistakes.

Mr. Brown: Can you use a computer?

Gina: Yes, I can. I can use several computer programs.

Mr. Brown: Can you speak Spanish?

Gina: No, I can't, but I understand it. I can speak Italian.

Mr. Brown: Can you work on weekends?

Gina: Oh, yes. In fact, a Saturday work schedule is better for me.

Mr. Brown: That's good. Do you have any questions?

Gina: Yes. How often do you need a secretary on weekends?

Mr. Brown: Almost every Saturday.

Have you ever had an interview? Tell the class about your experience.

1 She can speak Italian.

Pair Circle the letter of the statement that is true about Gina.

1. a. She can type.   b. She can't type.

2. a. She can speak Spanish.   b. She can't speak Spanish.

3. a. She can speak Italian.   b. She can't speak Italian.

4. a. She can use a computer.   b. She can't use a computer.

5. a. She seldom makes mistakes   b. She never makes mistakes when she types.
        when she types.

2 Word Bag: Occupations

Look at the pictures. Listen and read. Label each picture with an occupation from the list.

| architect pilot hairdresser doctor mail carrier police officer lawyer dentist |

I cut people's hair.
I always talk to my
customers.

I am a <u>hairdresser</u>.

I usually work in a
hospital. I make
people feel better.

I am a _____.

I am often in a
courthouse. I defend
people in court.

I am a _____.

I always work with a
team to build a
house.

I am an _____.

I carry letters and
packages in my bag.
I often talk to people
on the street.

I am a _____.

I am always ready to
help people.
I usually drive a car.

I am a _____.

I work on people's
teeth. I usually work
in my office.

I am a _____.

I spend most of my
time on the plane. I
always travel from
one place to another.

I am a _____.

Class One student pantomimes an occupation. The class guesses what it is by asking questions, for example, "Do you work in a hospital?" "Do you wear a uniform?"

3 Are Gina and Oscar a good match?

Gina and Oscar like each other. Are they a good match? Why or why not? Read the following.

Gina likes movies. She sees one **once a week**. She **seldom** stays home on weekends. She likes to go out with friends, and she **often** goes to parties. **Sometimes** she watches TV in the evening. She **never** exercises at the gym, but **sometimes** she swims in the school pool. She **sometimes** goes to concerts with friends.

Oscar likes movies and sports. He goes to the movies **once a week**. He often stays home on weekends. He likes to spend most of his time alone, and he **seldom** goes to parties. He **sometimes** watches TV in the evening. He goes to the gym **every day** after school, and he **sometimes** swims in the gym's pool. He **often** listens to classical music, but he never goes to concerts.

Write *G* for Gina and *O* for Oscar in the chart.

How often does Gina or Oscar	Always	Often	Sometimes	Seldom	Never	Once a week	Every day
watch movies?							
go to parties?							
exercise?							
go swimming?							
go to concerts?							

4 Find out more about a classmate.

Ask how often he or she does the activities below. Write a sentence for each activity on the line provided. Use the adverbs in the chart above.

Example: go to the mall
          Pam seldom goes to the mall.

1. exercise

   _____

2. watch TV late at night

   _____

3. take the bus to school

   _____

4. go swimming

   _____

5. come to class late

   _____

Lesson 3

In this lesson, you will learn to
- describe how people do things.
- ask how people do things.

Gina is a great worker!

Listen and read.

Gina is a secretary at a bank. She writes her boss's letters, does a lot of filing, works on the computer, and answers the phone. She works fast and answers the phone politely. She knows computers very well, and she does her filing carefully. She always dresses appropriately, and she never speaks rudely to her co-workers. She does her job very well. Her new boss likes her very much!

Group List Gina's office skills on the board. Discuss the importance of each skill. Then take a vote to choose the skill that is the most important to have as a secretary.

1 She's a polite person.

Pair Look at the pictures. Ask and answer questions. Use the words in the lists. Follow the example.

Example: careful driver

    A: Are you a *careful driver*?
    B: Yes, I am. I *drive carefully*.

Adjective	Adverb
good	well
fast	fast
hard	hard
bad	badly
slow	slowly
polite	politely

speak	sing	dance	work	jog	run

    polite speaker   bad singer   fast runner

    good dancer   hard worker   slow jogger

2 Information Gap Activity, pages 135 and 136.

Pair Turn to pages 135 and 136 and follow your teacher's instructions.

3 Online

 Log onto **http://www.prenhall.com/brown_activities**
The Web: This is my resume.
Grammar: What's your grammar IQ?
E-mail: Someday, I want to be . . .

4 Wrap Up

Group   Work in groups of three. Read the Help Wanted ad.

Complete the sentences with adverbs.

> **Drivers Needed**
>
> Are you looking for extra income?
> Can you drive _____?
> Do you speak English _____?
> Can you work long hours?

On a piece of paper, create a simple Help Wanted ad for one of these jobs:

| English tutor | nanny | waiter | cashier |

Share your ad with the class.

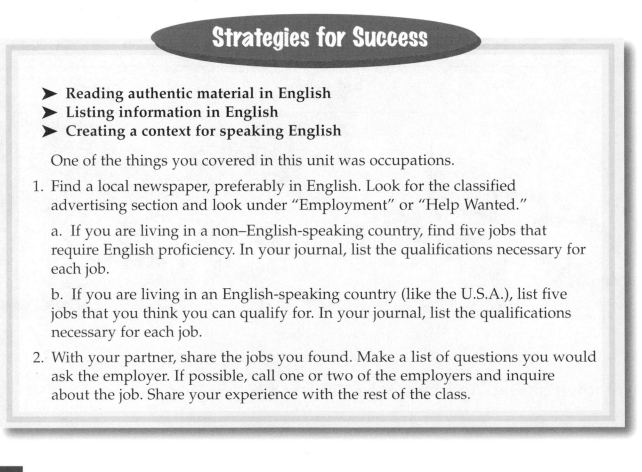

Strategies for Success

➤ **Reading authentic material in English**
➤ **Listing information in English**
➤ **Creating a context for speaking English**

One of the things you covered in this unit was occupations.

1. Find a local newspaper, preferably in English. Look for the classified advertising section and look under "Employment" or "Help Wanted."

   a. If you are living in a non–English-speaking country, find five jobs that require English proficiency. In your journal, list the qualifications necessary for each job.

   b. If you are living in an English-speaking country (like the U.S.A.), list five jobs that you think you can qualify for. In your journal, list the qualifications necessary for each job.

2. With your partner, share the jobs you found. Make a list of questions you would ask the employer. If possible, call one or two of the employers and inquire about the job. Share your experience with the rest of the class.

CHECKPOINT

I can	Yes!	Sometimes	Not Yet
fill out a job application form.	❑	❑	❑
ask and talk about abilities.	❑	❑	❑
talk about occupations.	❑	❑	❑
ask how often someone does an activity.	❑	❑	❑
ask and describe how people do things.	❑	❑	❑

Learning Preferences

Think about the work you did in this unit. Put a check (✓) next to the items that helped you learn the lessons. Put two checks next to the ones that helped a lot.

❑ ❑ Listening to the teacher
❑ ❑ Working by myself
❑ ❑ Working with a partner
❑ ❑ Working with a group
❑ ❑ Asking the teacher questions

❑ ❑ Listening to the tapes and doing exercises
❑ ❑ Reading
❑ ❑ Writing paragraphs
❑ ❑ Using the Internet

VOCABULARY

Occupations	Action Words	Other Vocabulary
architect	carry	appropriately
cashier	drive	co-worker
clerk	file	date of birth
dentist	fill out	degree
doctor	go over	fax machine
hairdresser	hire	gym
lawyer	play	interview
mail carrier	ride	nightshift
nanny	rollerblade	office skill
pilot	spend	once
police officer	type	packages
secretary		photocopy machine
tutor		place of birth
waiter		

Yes/No Questions Using *Can*

Helping Verb *Can*	Subject	Main Verb	Object
Can	she	**play**	basketball?

Short Response

Yes, she **can**. *or* No, she **can't**.

Adjectives and Adverbs of Manner

Adjectives	Adverbs
bad	bad**ly**
careful	careful**ly**
polite	polite**ly**
rude	rude**ly**
slow	slow**ly**

Adverbs of Frequency

How often does he exercise?

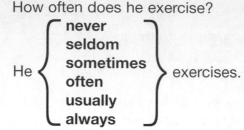

He { never / seldom / sometimes / often / usually / always } exercises.

He exercises **once a week/every day**.

Irregular Adjectives/Adverbs of Manner

Adjectives	Adverbs
good	well
fast	fast
hard	hard

► COMMUNICATION SUMMARY

Asking and talking about abilities
Can you use a computer?
　Yes, I can. I can use several programs.
Can you speak Spanish?
　No, I can't.

Talking about occupations
I cut people's hair. I'm a hairdresser.

Asking and talking about frequency
How often do you go to the movies?
　I go to the movies once a week.
　I never go to the movies.

Requesting and giving personal information at an interview
Can you tell me about yourself?
　I am a student. I sometimes work as my
　uncle's secretary.

Describing how people do things
Gina types fast.
She never speaks rudely to her co-workers.
I drive carefully.

UNIT 10

Lesson 1

In this lesson, you will learn to
- talk about past activities.
- talk about weekend activities.
- write a personal time line.
- talk about important events.

How was your weekend?

 Listen and read.

Tony: Hi, Lynn! How was your weekend?

Lynn: It was fun. I went out with friends.

Tony: What did you do?

Lynn: We went dancing and then out for a bite to eat. How was your weekend?

Tony: Oh, not very exciting. I just stayed home and watched TV on Saturday.

Lynn: Well, what did you do on Sunday?

Tony: Sunday was terrible! I waited all day for my girlfriend to call, but she didn't!

Circle the correct answer.

1.	Lynn had a good weekend.	True	False	Don't know
2.	Tony had a good weekend, too.	True	False	Don't know
3.	Lynn went to a restaurant.	True	False	Don't know
4.	Tony watched a movie on TV.	True	False	Don't know
5.	Tony called his girlfriend.	True	False	Don't know

Pair Did you have a fun weekend? Tell your partner how you spent your weekend.

1 Hear it. Say it.

Listen to the sounds of *-ed* at the end of each word.

Final *-ed*		
/t/ cooked	/d/ played	/ɪd/ painted

Listen to each word. Write the end sound that you hear. Then read each word aloud.

1. shouted / /
2. watched / /
3. listened / /

4. visited / /
5. cleaned / /
6. talked / /

7. danced / /
8. waited / /
9. stayed / /

2 I had a fun weekend.

Listen and read.

A: **Did** you **have** a nice weekend?

B: It **was** fun. I **visited** some friends. How **was** yours?

A: Oh, not very exciting. I **stayed** home and **watched** TV.

Present		Past
am, is		was
are		were
does	do	did
goes	go	went
has	have	had

Pair Read the conversation with a partner. Then fill in the blanks.

1. A: Was the weekend good?

   B: It _____ great! I (*dance*) _____ with my girlfriend all night Friday. How _____ yours?

   A: It _____ terrible. My boyfriend didn't call me.

2. A: What's the matter?

   B: I have a headache.

   A: A headache? How did you get it?

   B: I (*talk*) _____ on the telephone for an hour, I (*listen*) _____ to loud music, and I (*shout*) _____ at my dog.

3. A: How _____ your weekend?

   B: It _____ OK. I (*visit*) _____ some friends. They (*cook*) _____ dinner for me, and then we (*watch*) _____ an old movie on TV.

4. A: _____ you have a nice weekend?

   B: It _____ fun. I (*go*) _____ out with my classmates.

   A: Where did you go?

   B: We _____ (*go*) to the park and _____ (*talk*) all day.

3 What did you do last weekend?

Check (✓) the activities you did this past weekend.

( ) cut the lawn or worked in the garden

( ) watched TV or videos

( ) listened to music

( ) read or studied

( ) went to a movie, disco, or restaurant

( ) exercised or played sports

( ) visited family or friends

( ) went to a museum

( ) attended a free concert at the park

( ) went to a party or had dinner at a
       friend's house

( ) enjoyed a hobby, such as taking photos

( ) other: _____

Pair Show your answers to a classmate. Did you check any of the same activities? Discuss how you each spent the weekend.

4 Headline News

Listen to Oscar, Ivan, and Nelson talk about their weekends. Write the name of each person under the newspaper headline for his story.

_____

_____

_____

_____

5 Personal Time Line

Write down the five most important events in your life. Show when they happened. Record the events on your Personal Time Line. Look at Bill Gates's Time Line as an example.

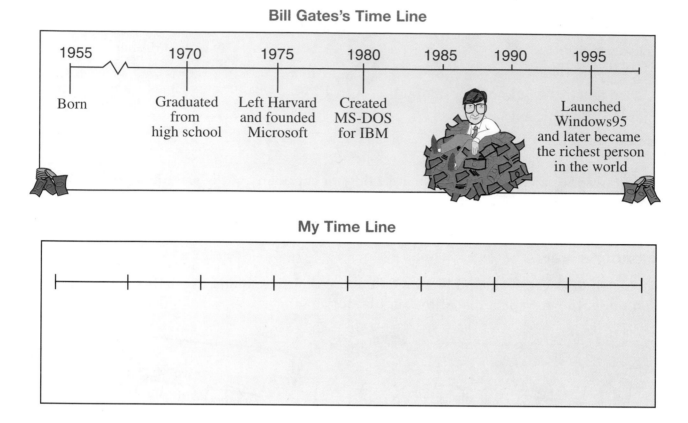

Bill Gates's Time Line

| 1955 | 1970 | 1975 | 1980 | 1985 | 1990 | 1995 |

Born — Graduated from high school — Left Harvard and founded Microsoft — Created MS-DOS for IBM — Launched Windows95 and later became the richest person in the world

My Time Line

Pair Show your Personal Time Line to your partner. Together, discuss the important events in your lives. In the chart below, write the four most important events in your partner's life.

	What was the event?	When did it happen?	Where did it happen?	How did he/she feel at the time?
1.				
2.				
3.				
4.				

Take turns telling what the most important year in your life was. Tell why it was the most important year in your life.

Lesson 2

In this lesson, you will learn to
- ask for and give change.
- give and follow directions.
- make a suggestion.
- order in a restaurant.

How do you use this machine?

🔊 **Listen and read.**

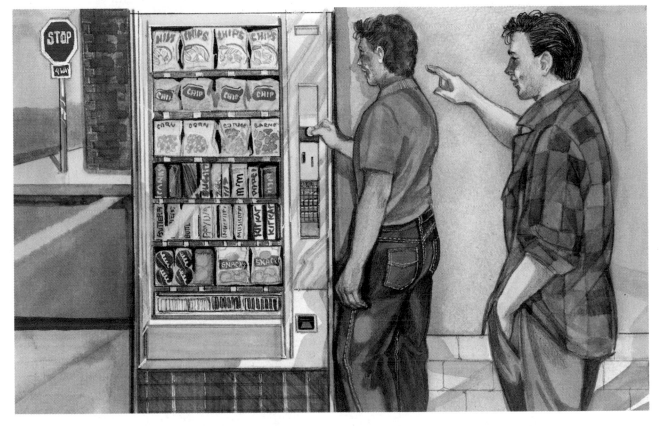

Tony: Oscar, how do you use this machine?

Oscar: I'll show you. First, decide what you want.

Tony: I want some cookies.

Oscar: Cookies are fifty cents. Do you have any change?

Tony: I have a quarter, two dimes, and five pennies.

Oscar: You can't use the pennies. Here's a nickel.

Tony: Thanks. Let's see now. I put the coins in here, right?

Oscar: Right. Then press the button for cookies.

Tony: That's easy. Want a cookie?

Oscar: No, thanks. Hey, you owe me a nickel!

<u>Pair</u> Find a machine (a computer, a copier, a vending machine, or a fax machine) in your school. Tell your partner how to use it.

1 Make your selection.

Look at the pictures. Fill in the blanks.

1. Make your selection.
2. Insert the _____.
   Don't use _____.
3. Press the correct _____.
4. Remove the _____.

1. Make _____ _____.
2. _____ the coins.
   _____ _____ pennies.
3. _____ the correct button.
4. _____ the soda.

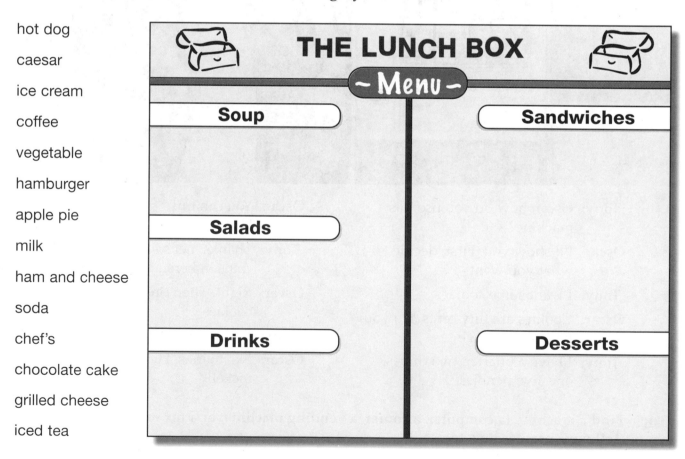 Listen.

Pair Now, tell your partner how to use the stamp machine.

2 Word Bag: Food and Drink

Write the words on the left in the correct category on the menu.

hot dog

caesar

ice cream

coffee

vegetable

hamburger

apple pie

milk

ham and cheese

soda

chef's

chocolate cake

grilled cheese

iced tea

THE LUNCH BOX
~Menu~

Soup

Sandwiches

Salads

Drinks

Desserts

3 Let's get something to eat.

Read the ad. Then listen and read the conversation.

The Star Restaurant
Great sandwiches
Open from
11:30 A.M. to 11:30 P.M.
107 North St.

Oscar: Would you like to get something to eat?

Tony: Good idea. Where do you want to eat?

Oscar: How about the Star Restaurant? They have great sandwiches.

Tony: How late is it open?

Oscar: Until 11:30 P.M.

Tony: Where is it?

Oscar: Over on North Street, next to the public library.

Pair Invite your partner to go somewhere or to do something, such as have dinner on Friday night, watch a movie, or play soccer. Write your dialog on a piece of paper and present it to the class.

4 Are you ready to order?

Read the menu below. Then listen and read the conversation.

```
★★★  STAR RESTAURANT MENU  ★★★
             TODAY'S SPECIAL
Soup and sandwich with salad or French fries  $6.95
```

SANDWICHES		SALADS	
Chicken	$3.95	House large	$4.50
Egg salad	$3.25	small	$2.25
Tuna salad	$4.50	Caesar	$4.00
Hamburger	$3.95	Chef	$6.50
Cheeseburger	$4.50	**SOUP**	
Grilled cheese	$3.25	**Vegetable/Chicken**	
DRINKS		Bowl	$3.25
Coffee	$1.00	Cup	$1.85
Tea	$.75	**DESSERTS**	
Milk	$.95	**Ice Cream**	$2.00
Soda large	$1.50	Chocolate/Vanilla/Strawberry	
medium	$.95	**Pie** (per slice)	$2.50
small	$.75	Apple or Cherry	
		Cake (per slice)	$3.00
		Chocolate or Carrot	

A: Are you ready to order?

B: Yes, I'd like *a chicken sandwich* and *a cup of soup*, please.

A: Would you like *chicken* or *vegetable soup*?

B: *Vegetable*, please.

A: Anything to drink?

B: I'd like *a soda*, please.

A: *Small, medium,* or *large*?

B: *Medium*, please.

A: Anything else?

B: Yes. *A slice of apple pie.*

Pair Role play a restaurant scene. Your partner will be the waiter. Order your lunch. Choose from the menu above.

5 Information Gap Activity, pages 137 and 138.

Pair Turn to pages 137 and 138 and follow your teacher's instructions.

Lesson 3

In this lesson, you will learn to
- extend an invitation.
- accept an invitation.
- refuse an invitation.
- make future plans.

School's almost over!

Listen and read.

Gina: What are you going to do during the school break?

Tony: I'm going to Florida. My uncle sent me a plane ticket. I'm really thrilled! I'm going to the beach with all my cousins. What about you? Are you staying here, or are you going away?

Gina: I'm going to attend a seminar in New York. My employer is sending me.

Tony: That's great! Are you excited?

Gina: Yes, I want to see the big city.

Tony: When are you leaving?

Gina: Next Monday.

Tony: By the way, some of us are having a picnic tomorrow. We're going to celebrate the end of the course. Would you like to come?

Gina: I'd love to. Thanks.

Pair What are you going to do on your summer vacation? Tell your partner about it.

1 Word Bag: Leisure Activities

Pair Write each activity in the appropriate column on the chart.

art show
barbecue
soccer match
concert

fishing
camping
a stage play
beach party

a musical
amusement park
football game
picnic

car show
basketball game
museum

Sporting Events	Live Performances	Exhibitions	Gatherings with Friends

Add two more activities to each list.

2 Invitations

Listen to the conversations. Then listen again and draw a line to connect the invitation in Column A with the response in Column B.

Column A

1. I'm going fishing this weekend. Would you like to come?

2. What are you going to do this evening? Do you want to see a movie?

3. We're having a picnic on Sunday. Can you join us?

4. Nelson's going to have some friends over on Friday. Would you like to come?

Column B

a. I can't. I have to babysit for my brother.

b. I'd love to. He has the best parties.

c. Sure. Can you lend me a fishing rod?

d. Sorry. We're going to drive to San Diego for the day.

Pair Choose an activity from the invitations above. Invite a classmate to go with you. Your partner can accept the invitation or refuse it.

3 What are you going to do during the break?

Group Interview three classmates and find out what they are going to do during the semester break. Share their plans with the class.

Examples:

A: What *are you going to do* during the break, Lynn?
B: *I'm going to* visit my aunt in Illinois.

A: What about you, Oscar?
C: *I'm going to* look for a job.

4 Online

Log onto **http://www.prenhall.com/brown_activities**
The Web: Let's make a time capsule.
Grammar: What's your grammar IQ?
E-mail: Dear friend: Good-bye . . .
    Dear teacher: Being online was . . .

5 Wrap Up

Group Ask your classmates what they did last weekend and what they will do next weekend.

Examples:

A: What did you do last weekend, Tony?
B: I *studied* for my test.

A: And what are you going to do this weekend?
B: I'm going to go to *the beach*!

Name	Last Weekend	Next Weekend
1.		
2.		
3.		
4.		

Strategies for Success

➤ **Writing about familiar information**
➤ **Creating authentic contexts for speaking and listening to English**

You have been looking at time lines and restaurant menus.

1. In your journal, write a brief autobiography (story of your life). Include as many details as you can.

2. (a) In non-English-speaking countries, go with your partner and some classmates to a restaurant where the staff speaks English. Ask for an English menu. Use only English to order your food and to pay the bill. While you're there, speak only English with your classmates.

    (b) In English-speaking countries, go with your partner and some other classmates to a restaurant, order food, and pay the bill, all in English. While you're there, speak only English with your classmates.

3. Recycle your strategies: go through all the strategies in this book and pick three favorites. Practice those strategies when you finish this course in English.

CHECKPOINT

I can	Yes!	Sometimes	Not Yet
talk about past activities.	❑	❑	❑
write a personal time line.	❑	❑	❑
talk about important events.	❑	❑	❑
ask for and make change.	❑	❑	❑
give and follow directions.	❑	❑	❑
make a suggestion.	❑	❑	❑
order in a restaurant.	❑	❑	❑
extend an invitation.	❑	❑	❑
accept or refuse an invitation.	❑	❑	❑
make future plans.	❑	❑	❑

Learning Preferences

Think about the work you did in this unit. Put a check (✓) next to the items that helped you learn the lessons. Put two checks next to the ones that helped a lot.

❑ ❑ Listening to the teacher
❑ ❑ Working by myself
❑ ❑ Working with a partner
❑ ❑ Working with a group
❑ ❑ Asking the teacher questions

❑ ❑ Listening to the tapes and doing exercises
❑ ❑ Reading
❑ ❑ Writing paragraphs
❑ ❑ Using the Internet

VOCABULARY

Food

apple pie	hamburger
cheeseburger	salad
cherry pie	sandwich
chocolate cake	strawberry
dessert	tuna
French fries	vanilla
grilled cheese	

Action Words

attend	press
cook	remove
decide	stay
go away	try (to)
insert	wait
leave	watch
miss	visit
order	

► GRAMMAR SUMMARY

Past Tense: Regular Verbs
Did you **stay** home last weekend?
No, I **visited** some friends. They **cooked** dinner, and we **watched** TV.

Future: *Be going to* + verb
What **are** you **going to** do during the school break?
I**'m going to** look for a job.
I**'m going to** attend a seminar.
What **are** you **going to** do this evening?
I**'m** not **going to** do anything. *or* Nothing.

Past Tense: Irregular Verbs
How **was** your weekend?
It **was** great.
Where **did** you **go**?
We **went** to a movie.

Expressions of Future Time
later
tomorrow
tonight
next week
this weekend
after class
during the (next) school break

► COMMUNICATION SUMMARY

Asking for change
Do you have change for a dollar?
Yes. Here you are.
Thanks.
Do you have change for a five?
No, I don't. Sorry.
Thanks anyway.

Making suggestions
Let's get something to eat.
Good idea.
How about the Star Restaurant? They have great sandwiches.
That's fine.

Talking about the future
What are you going to do this weekend?
I'm going to the beach.

Ordering in a restaurant
Are you ready to order?
Yes. I'd like a chicken sandwich.
I'd like a soda, please.

► GAMES AND ACTIVITIES

Information Gap Activity

Look at the four pictures. You have some information about the people. Your partner (Student B) also has some information about them. Find out the information that is missing, and write it in your book. Don't look at your partner's page!

	1		**2**
Name	Sara Souza		
Country			Vietnam
Course			English 1

	3		**4**
Name	Anna Bushinski		
Country			Japan
Course	English 4		

Useful Language

Who is the person *in picture 2*?   *He's/She's* . . .
Where is *he/she* from?   *He's/She's* from . . .
What course is *he/she* in?   *He's/She's* in . . .

Unit 1 Blackline Master **121**

Information Gap Activity ✏️ **Student B**

Look at the four pictures. You have some information about the people. Your partner (Student A) also has some information about them. Find out the information that is missing, and write it in your book. Don't look at your partner's page!

	1		**2**
Name	_____		Martin Ha
Country	Brazil		_____
Course	English 1		_____

	3		**4**
Name	_____		Michio Tanaka
Country	Russia		_____
Course	_____		English

Useful Language

Who is the person *in picture 1*?   *He's/She's . . .*
Where is *he/she* from?   *He's/She's from . . .*
What course is *he/she* in?   *He's/She's in . . .*

122 **Unit 1 Blackline Master**   © 1999 Prentice Hall Regents. Duplication for classroom use is permitted.

Concentration

1	2	3	4	5
6	7	8	9	10
11	12	13	14	15
16	17	18	19	20
30	40	50	60	70

sixty	five	nineteen	sixteen	seven
eight	fourteen	fifty	ten	seventeen
twelve	twenty	nine	thirty	two
eleven	six	seventy	one	eighteen
thirteen	three	forty	fifteen	four

Unit 2 Blackline Master

Relative Name Tags

The Solo Family Tree

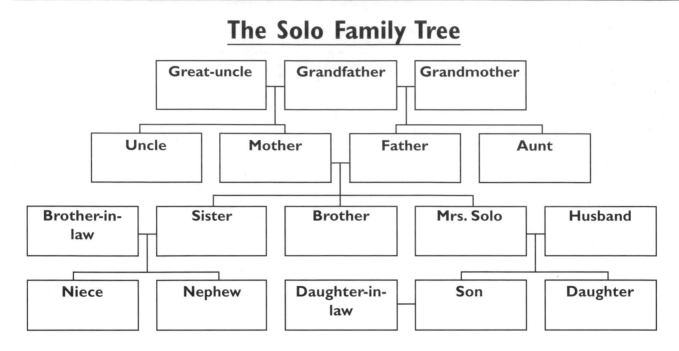

Relative Name Tags

Mrs. Solo's Grandfather

Mrs. Solo's Grandmother

Mrs. Solo's Great-uncle

Mrs. Solo's Uncle

Mrs. Solo's Mother

Mrs. Solo's Father

Mrs. Solo's Aunt

Mrs. Solo's Brother-in-law

Mrs. Solo's Sister

Mrs. Solo's Brother

Mrs. Solo's Husband

Mrs. Solo's Niece

Mrs. Solo's Nephew

Mrs. Solo's Daughter-in-law

Mrs. Solo's Son

Mrs. Solo's Daughter

Information Gap Activity

Look at the map below. Some of the place names are missing. Find out what's missing by listening to your partner's description of the map. Write the missing names in the appropriate places on the map. Don't look at Student B's page!

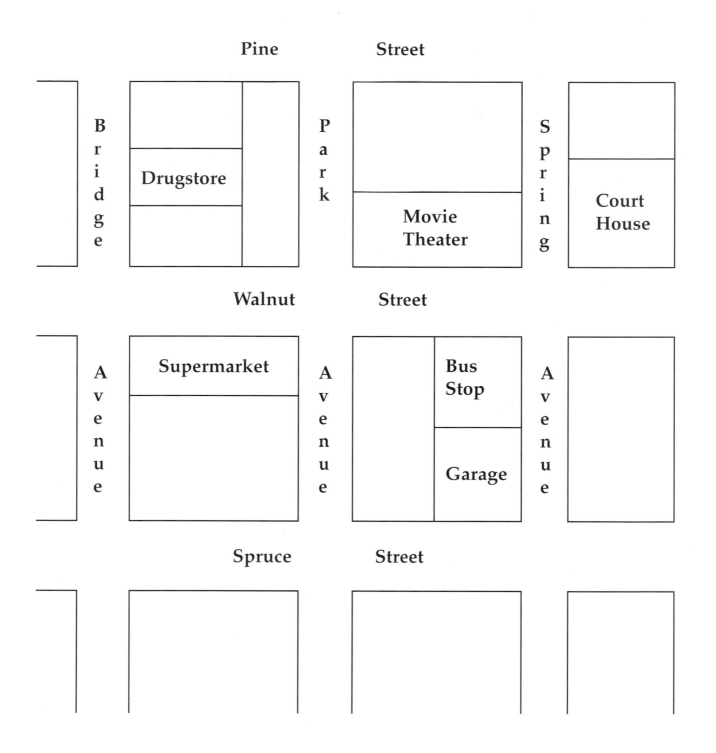

Unit 4 Blackline Master 125

Information Gap Activity

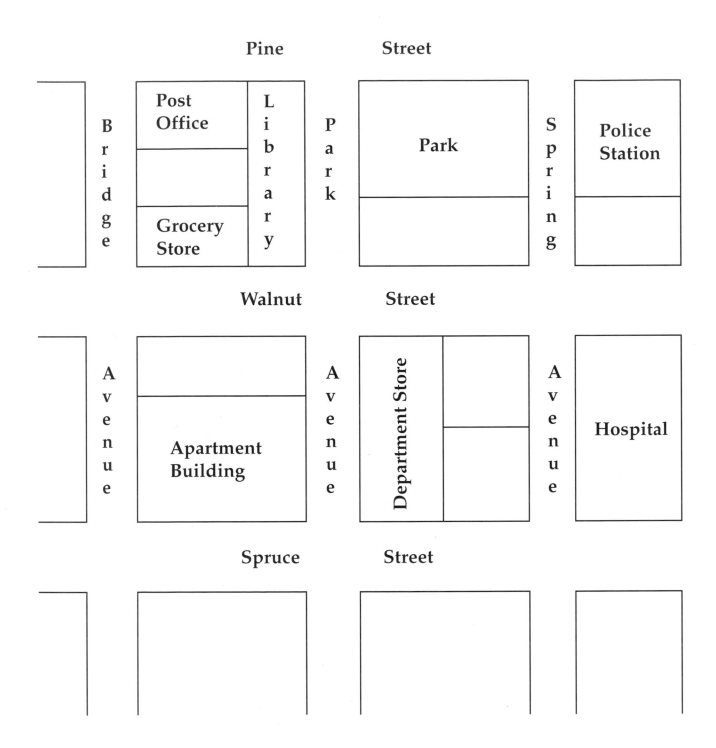

Student B

Look at the map below. Some of the place names are missing. Find out what's missing by listening to your partner's description of the map. Write the missing names in the appropriate places on the map. Don't look at Student A's page!

Pine　　　　Street

Bridge

Post Office

Library

Grocery Store

Park

Park

Spring

Police Station

Walnut　　　Street

Avenue

Apartment Building

Avenue

Department Store

Avenue

Hospital

Spruce　　　Street

Information Gap Activity ✏️

Look at the weather key below. It contains symbols for different weather conditions. The map shows weather conditions in four different regions. Find out what the weather is like in the remaining three regions by asking your partner questions. Don't look at Student B's book! Add the appropriate symbols to your map. Check your information by showing your partner your book.

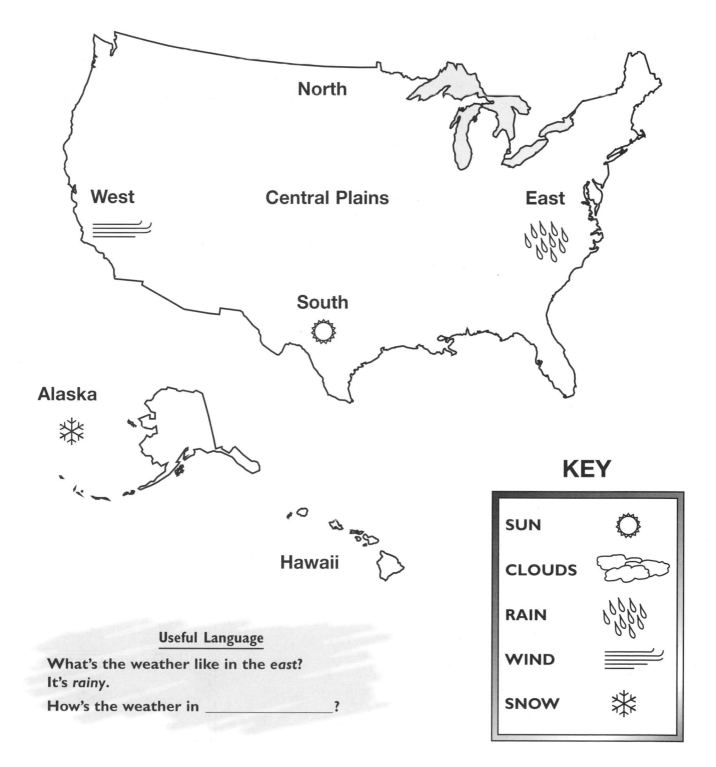

KEY

SUN	☀️
CLOUDS	☁️
RAIN	🌧️
WIND	〰️
SNOW	❄️

Useful Language

What's the weather like in the *east*?
It's *rainy*.
How's the weather in _____?

Information Gap Activity Student B

Look at the weather key below. It contains symbols for different weather conditions. The map shows weather conditions in four different regions. Find out what the weather is like in the remaining three regions by asking your partner questions. Don't look at your partner's book! Add the appropriate symbols to your map. Check your information by showing your partner your book.

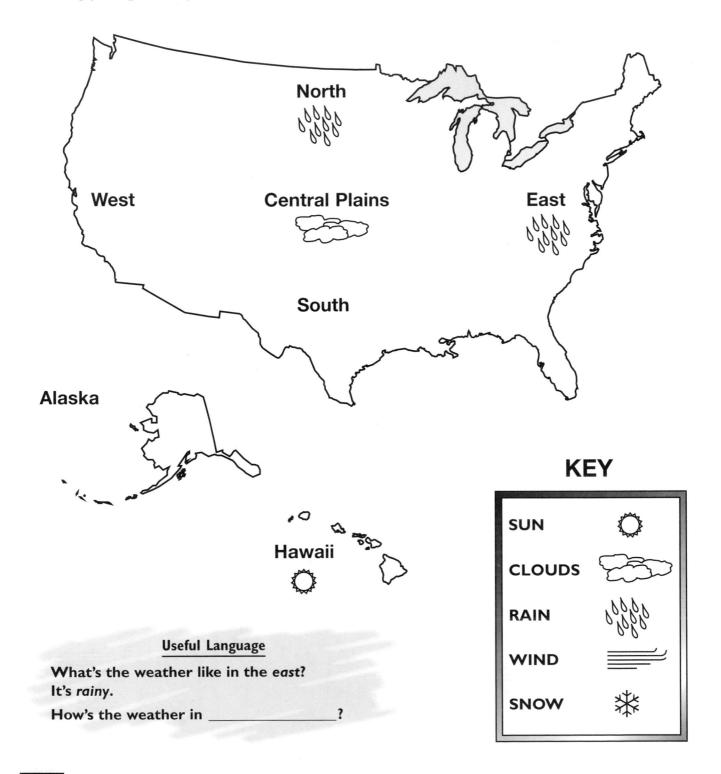

North

West

Central Plains

East

South

Alaska

Hawaii

KEY

SUN	
CLOUDS	
RAIN	
WIND	
SNOW	

Useful Language

What's the weather like in the *east*?
It's *rainy*.
How's the weather in _____?

Information Gap Activity

Student A

Write your schedule for next week. Write eight things you want to do in your schedule. Invite your partner to do these things with you. Make changes in your schedule if necessary.

	Morning	Afternoon	Evening
Sunday			
Monday			
Tuesday			
Wednesday			
Thursday			
Friday			
Saturday			

Useful Language

A: What do you do on *Sunday morning*?
B: Nothing. I get up late.
A: Do you want to *go jogging*?
B: Sure.
   No, I don't. How about in *the afternoon*?

Information Gap Activity

Write your schedule for next week. Write eight things you want to do in your schedule. Invite your partner to do these things with you. Make changes in your schedule if necessary.

	Morning	Afternoon	Evening
Sunday			
Monday			
Tuesday			
Wednesday			
Thursday			
Friday			
Saturday			

Useful Language

A: What do you do on *Sunday morning*?
B: Nothing. I get up late.
A: Do you want to *go jogging*?
B: Sure.
   No, I don't. How about in *the afternoon*?

Information Gap Activity

Look at the food in your grocery store. Look at the shopping list of the food you want to buy in your partner's grocery store. Visit your partner's grocery store and ask for the food on your list. Don't look at your partner's page!

This is YOUR grocery store.

This is YOUR shopping list.

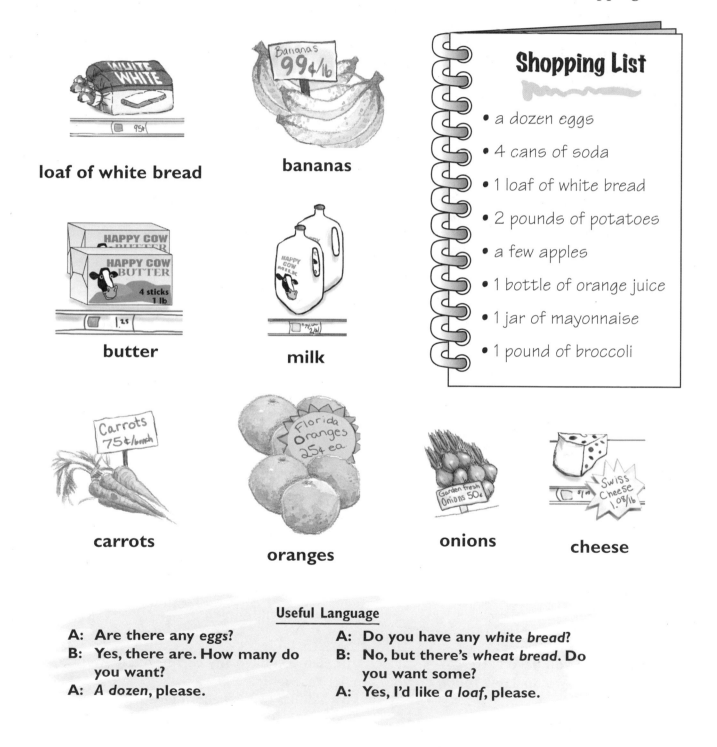

loaf of white bread

bananas

butter

milk

Shopping List

- a dozen eggs
- 4 cans of soda
- 1 loaf of white bread
- 2 pounds of potatoes
- a few apples
- 1 bottle of orange juice
- 1 jar of mayonnaise
- 1 pound of broccoli

carrots

oranges

onions

cheese

Useful Language

A: Are there any *eggs*?
B: Yes, there are. How many do you want?
A: *A dozen*, please.

A: Do you have any *white bread*?
B: No, but there's *wheat bread*. Do you want some?
A: Yes, I'd like *a loaf*, please.

Information Gap Activity

Look at the food in your grocery store. Look at the shopping list of the food you want to buy in your partner's grocery store. Visit your partner's grocery store and ask for the food on your list. Don't look at your partner's page!

This is YOUR grocery store.

This is YOUR shopping list.

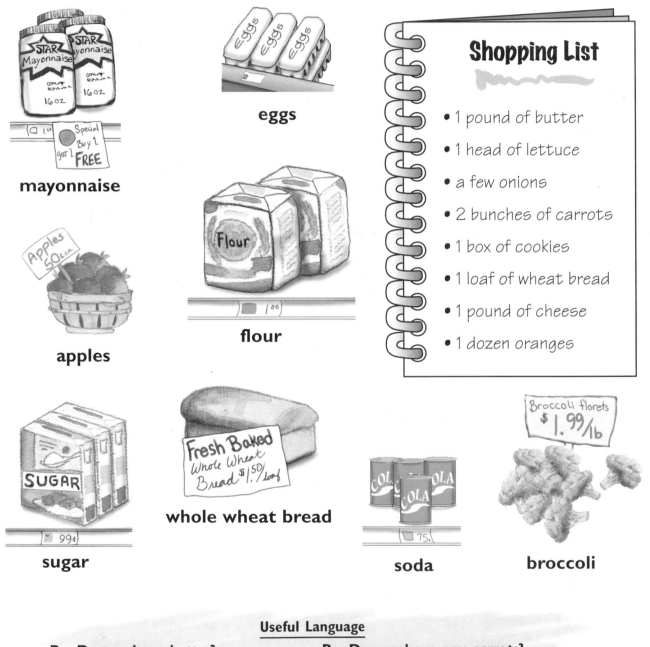

mayonnaise

eggs

apples

flour

Shopping List

- 1 pound of butter
- 1 head of lettuce
- a few onions
- 2 bunches of carrots
- 1 box of cookies
- 1 loaf of wheat bread
- 1 pound of cheese
- 1 dozen oranges

sugar

whole wheat bread

soda

broccoli

Useful Language

B: **Do you have** *butter*?
A: **Yes, we do. How much do you need?**
B: *A pound*, **please.**

B: **Do you have any** *carrots*?
A: **Yes we do.**
B: **I'd like** *two* **bunches please.**

Information Gap Activity

Student A

You and your friend are in New York City. You want to go to Ellis Island and see the Statue of Liberty together. Make an appointment with each other. Write it on your calendar. Don't look at your partner's page!

MONDAY

A.M.		P.M.	
9:00	Aunt Mary	1:00	Movies
10:00		2:00	↓
11:00	Cousin Bob	3:00	↓
12:00		4:00	

TUESDAY

A.M.		P.M.	
9:00		1:00	↓ Shop
10:00		2:00	Bank
11:00	Shop	3:00	Hair Salon
12:00	↓	4:00	

WEDNESDAY

A.M.		P.M.	
9:00	Midtown	1:00	
10:00		2:00	Museums w/ cousins
11:00	Empire State Building	3:00	↓
12:00		4:00	↓

THURSDAY

A.M.		P.M.	
9:00		1:00	
10:00	Call Chris	2:00	
11:00		3:00	
12:00		4:00	

FRIDAY

A.M.		P.M.	
9:00	West Point	1:00	Family get–together
10:00	↓	2:00	
11:00	↓	3:00	
12:00	↓	4:00	↓

Useful Language

A: Do you want to go to Ellis Island with me?
B: I'd love to.
A: When do you want to go?
B: How about Tuesday?

A: What time?
B: After two P.M.
A: Sorry. I can't.

You and your friend are in New York City. You want to go to Ellis Island and see the Statue of Liberty together. Make an appointment with each other. Write it on your calendar. Don't look at your partner's page!

MONDAY

A.M.		P.M.	
9:00	Breakfast w/ cousin	1:00	
10:00	Grandma	2:00	
11:00		3:00	Visit Molly in Hospital
12:00	LUNCH	4:00	↓

TUESDAY

9:00	Aunt Alice	1:00	Uncle Richard
10:00	Cousin Ed	2:00	
11:00		3:00	
12:00	LUNCH	4:00	Sam

WEDNESDAY

9:00	Museum w/ Mom	1:00	Shop with Mom
10:00	↓	2:00	
11:00	↓	3:00	
12:00	LUNCH	4:00	↓

THURSDAY

9:00	Wait for overseas call	1:00	
10:00	Post office	2:00	
11:00		3:00	
12:00		4:00	

FRIDAY

9:00		1:00	LUNCH
10:00	Midtown	2:00	
11:00	↓	3:00	Broadway
12:00	↓	4:00	↓

Useful Language

B: Do you want to go to Ellis Island with me?

A: I'd love to.

B: When do you want to go?

A: How about Wednesday?

B: What time?

A: At one P.M.

B: Sorry. I can't.

Information Gap Activity

Look at the list of candidates for a job. Read what the interviewers think of each candidate. You have one interviewer's complete rating and another's partial rating. Complete the ratings for all of the candidates by asking your partner questions. Write the ratings in your book. On a scale* of 1 to 10, decide on a final mark to give each candidate. Write the final mark in the last column. Don't look at your partner's page!

*10=excellent   7=very good   5=good   3=average   1=poor

	Mr. Brown	Mrs. Black	Ms. White	Final Mark
John	average			
Paul	excellent			
Mary	excellent		very good	
Selena	poor		good	
Mario	good			
Linda	poor		poor	

Useful Language

A: **What does *Mrs. Black* think about *John*?**
B: **She thinks he's *very good*. What does *Mr. Brown* think?**
A: **He doesn't agree. He thinks *John* is *average*.**

Who gets the job?

Information Gap Activity

Look at the list of candidates for a job. Read what the interviewers think of each candidate. You have one interviewer's complete rating and another's partial rating. Complete the ratings for all of the candidates by asking your partner questions. Write the ratings in your book. On a scale* of 1 to 10, decide on a final mark to give each candidate. Write the final mark in the last column. Don't look at your partner's page!

*10=excellent   7=very good   5=good   3=average   1=poor

	Mrs. Black	Mr. Brown	Ms. White	Final Mark
Selena	poor			
Mario	average		good	
Mary	average			
John	very good		average	
Linda	average			
Paul	very good		excellent	

Useful Language

B: What does *Mr. Brown* think about *John*?
A: He thinks he's *average.* What does *Mrs. Black* think?
B: She doesn't agree. She thinks *John* is *very good.*

Who gets the job?

Information Gap Activity

Student A

Read the menus below. One shows the prices; the other doesn't. Ask your partner questions to find out the missing prices. Write the prices on the menu. Don't look at your partner's page!

The Village Snack Bar

Drinks

Glass of milk	$0.50
Lemonade	$0.55
Coca-Cola	$0.75
Cup of coffee	$1.00
with cream	$1.05
Cup of tea	$0.55

Sandwiches

Hamburger	$1.25
Hot Dog	$0.99
Tuna	$1.30
Ham and Cheese	$1.50
Egg Salad	$1.35

Desserts

Apple Pie	$0.75
Chocolate Cake	$1.50
Ice Cream	$0.75

The Lunch Box Cafe

Drinks

Orangeade	
Pepsi-Cola	
Cup of coffee with ceam	
Cup of tea	
Glass of milk	

Sandwiches

Grilled Cheese	
Cheeseburger	
Chicken Salad	
Ham	
Egg Salad	

Desserts

Lemon Pie	
Carrot Cake	
Ice Cream	

Which restaurant is cheaper?

Useful Language

A: How much is *a cup of coffee?*

B: It's *ninety-five cents.* or *Ninety-five cents.*

Look at the two menus below. One shows the prices; the other doesn't. Ask your partner questions to find out the missing prices. Write the prices on the menu. Don't look at your partner's page!

The Village Snack Bar

Drinks

Glass of milk
Lemonade
Coca-Cola
Cup of coffee
    with cream
Cup of tea

Sandwiches

Hamburger
Hot Dog
Tuna
Ham and Cheese
Egg Salad

Desserts

Apple Pie
Chocolate Cake
Ice Cream

The Lunch Box Cafe

Drinks

Orangeade	$0.45
Pepsi-Cola	$0.70
Cup of coffee	$0.95
with cream	$1.00
Cup of tea	$0.50
Glass of milk	$0.45

Sandwiches

Grilled Cheese	$1.15
Cheeseburger	$1.25
Chicken Salad	$1.15
Ham	$1.25
Egg Salad	$1.30

Desserts

Lemon Pie	$0.65
Carrot Cake	$0.99
Ice Cream	$0.70

Which restaurant is cheaper?

Useful Language

B: How much is *a cup of coffee*?
A: It's *$1.00.* or A *dollar.*